Editor
Dona Herweck Rice

Editorial Project Manager
Ina Massler Levin, M.A.

Editor-in-Chief
Sharon Coan, M.S. Ed.

Illustrator
Agi Palinay

Cover Artist
Cheri Macoubrie Wilson

Art Coordinator
Cheri Macoubrie Wilson

Creative Director
Elayne Roberts

Imaging
Ralph Olmedo, Jr.

Product Manager
Phil Garcia

Publishers:
Rachelle Cracchiolo, M.S. Ed.
Mary Dupuy Smith, M.S. Ed.

How to Manage Your Early Childhood Classroom

Technology
Field Trips
Inclusion
Parent Conferences

Free Play
Year-End Programs
Health & Safety
Fine/Gross Motor Skills

Snack Time
Classroom Ideas
Patterns
Developmental Checklist

Art/Music
Circle Time
Behavior
Lesson Plans

Author:

Kathleen Thayer, M.A., and Susan Westby

Teacher Created Materials, Inc.
6421 Industry Way
Westminster, CA 92683
www.teachercreated.com

©*1999 Teacher Created Materials, Inc.*
Reprinted, 2004
Made in U.S.A.
ISBN-1-57690-324-9

Table of Contents

Introduction 4

The Classroom 5

What Every Teacher Needs to Know 24

Health and Safety 45

Developmental Checklists 66

Planning Lessons 92

Gross Motor Play 131

Fine Motor Play 140

Sensory Integration Play 145

Free Play 157

Snack Time 168

Art 176

Music 183

Circle Time 196

Field Trips 202

Behavior 210

Parent Conferences 226

Inclusion 233

Technology 244

Graduation and Year-End Programs 256

    Heigh Ho, Heigh Ho, It's Off to Camp We Go! 258

    Gift of Wings 267

    Music in Me 276

Awards 287

Patterns 290

Bibliography of Additional Resources 302

Index 303

What are we doing here? We're reaching for the stars.

—Christa McAuliffe

Introduction

Clearly, the preschool years are very important. Research tells us that the first five years of a child's life impact his learning potential for the rest of his life. Our purpose in creating this book is to provide preschool teachers with a means to ensure that their children are provided with the most enriching environment possible.

The whole-child and sensory approaches in this book are predicated on the idea that children will use every aspect of their senses and bodies to learn about the world in which we live. A teacher who picks up this manual will have a usable reference source that is all inclusive. In general, few adaptations are necessary for those children who have special needs. The encouraged approach is to teach children the same, as children. Of course, our goal as teachers is to do what is necessary to make each child successful. That is the basis for this book.

All material here has been class tested. Children from ages two to five have completed these activities successfully and with ease.

This book will give you, the teacher, the tools and information needed to begin your preschool year on a positive note and to keep it running effectively from the first day until summer vacation. Provided within these pages are ideas on planning, organizing your classroom, developmental guidelines, handling behavior, setting up schedules and conferences, health and safety issues, issues on inclusion of children with special needs, and several ideas for an end-of-the-year program your families will talk about for years to come! Also included are the what, where, and why of the preschool curriculum. A preschool teacher cannot be fully prepared without insight into these three questions. Finally, most sections of this book end with a page provided so that you can add notes of your own on each topic as well as the ideas you learn from your colleagues. In this way, you can keep all the information you need together in one place.

A well-prepared teacher, classroom, and materials are imperative for having a successful year. A preschool teacher may not see the results of her efforts for many months, but rest assured that everything the teacher does influences each child for a lifetime. Teaching preschool is an experience that will change your life.

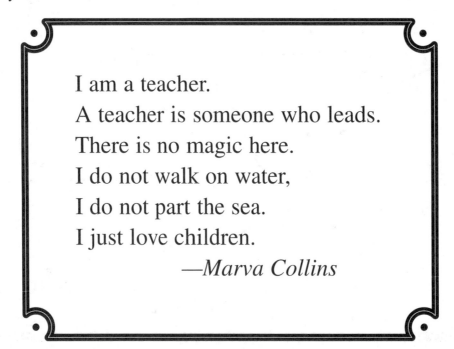

I am a teacher.
A teacher is someone who leads.
There is no magic here.
I do not walk on water,
I do not part the sea.
I just love children.
—*Marva Collins*

A classroom is a place with four walls with tomorrow inside.

—*Claudia Lesman Boysen*

Classroom Floor Plans

For the most part, your floor plan is at the mercy of the physical classroom you are given by your administrator. However, what you do with that space says a great deal about you as a professional. Parents and administrators may take their first impressions of you from your classroom before you have an opportunity to speak with them. Your room is a reflection of you.

A good floor plan is one in which you can see the learning areas clearly when you walk into the room. Ultimately, you are in control of not only the floor plan but also the traffic pattern of your classroom. The traffic pattern refers to the places in the room throughout which the children and teachers will move. The traffic pattern sets the tone of the room just as much as the wall decorations can, and it will likewise set the tone for activities and behaviors throughout the day.

When thinking about your overall classroom design, you should consider the accessibility of materials. The age of the children should be the first consideration. Children will use and play with whatever is accessible to them. Remember: If they see it, they will use it. Materials that are messy or toys with many pieces should be placed in an adult-only access area such as a high shelf or locked cabinet which the children cannot reach.

Accessibility in an organized fashion can be achieved in a manner which makes cleanup part of the child's play. These include grouping and matching like toys. Children can learn organizational skills by returning the toys to their storage areas. There are many ways to do this with young children.

Pictures: Label your shelves with a picture of the item next to where it is located. When using tubs, put the picture on the lid and on the inside of the bucket for easy matching.

Color coding: Use colors and shapes to indicate location or parts of toys that go together. This works better with older children who can match items together such as tapes and books.

Shadow Matting: Items such as kitchen playthings, dress-up clothing, and block-tubs are easily traced on colored paper or colored adhesive film and put underneath the object to create its shadow. The child matches the object with the shadow (colored mat). There is a one-to-one relationship between the item and its shadow.

Basket Cleanup: This kind of cleanup is great for even the youngest child. Place a basket in the middle of the floor area to be cleaned, and encourage the children to place the toys in the basket. Teachers and assistants can put the toys away after class time.

A neatly organized room will put everyone at ease. This is evident as soon as you open the classroom door. You can feel the magic or the chaos. We all want to feel the magic in our own space and classroom atmosphere.

Classroom Design and Decorations

Themes

Decorations make a classroom inviting. Theme decorating works well and is easy to maintain. You can easily hand-make the decorations or purchase them through your local school supply vendor. Choose a theme which you can change and/or keep year to year.

Here are some suggestions for themes:

Apples	*Dinosaurs*	*Mice*	*Stars and Stripes*
Balloons	*Fall*	*Mittens*	*Summer*
Bears	*Fish*	*Penguins*	*Sunflowers*
Birds	*Frogs*	*Rainbows*	*Suns*
Bunnies	*Hats*	*Shapes*	*Trains*
Butterflies	*Holidays*	*Snow*	*Winter*
Cars	*Homes*	*Space*	
Cats	*Kites*	*Spring*	

Use the themes you have chosen for all your classroom decorations, newsletters, incentives, and announcements.

An example of this total theme idea is shown here. Use the theme to put pictures of the children in a classroom roll call on the wall. A welcome sign on the door with the theme logo is a very nice touch. At the spots where the children sit, you can put the logo with each of their names on it. This not only looks attractive, but it also helps the children to recognize their names many times throughout the day. Finally, your unit of study can always be incorporated into the theme.

Classroom Design and Decorations (cont.)

"Lowering" the Ceiling

It is important to hang items from the ceiling. This gives a sense of security to very young children who spend an enormous amount of time on the floor. To little people, an eight-foot ceiling seems very high. The younger the child, the more important a lower ceiling is.

An easy method to use for hanging items is with clear fishing line and a paper clip. Tie the line to the paper clip and bend the clip to slide into the ceiling divider panels. If your ceiling is not a dropped ceiling, use the line and clear tape to secure it to the ceiling. Also, do not let safety slip your mind. Use a good steady ladder and a helper if necessary to get the job done. Safety first!

Toy Inventory

A well-arranged classroom is also stacked with age-appropriate toys. Below is a checklist of standard items you may want to purchase or ask to be donated. (An extended checklist can be found on pages 13–15.)

- cooking utensils
- cooking pots
- toy refrigerator
- toy sink
- toy stove
- toy cupboard
- puppets

- small table and chairs
- colorful stacking blocks
- wooden puzzles
- large, soft balls
- dolls
- cars and trucks

Centers

On pages 17–19 you will find center area signs which you can reproduce and laminate to use in your classroom. Before laminating, it is useful to color them to make them attractive for the children. The more appealing they are, the more likely the children are to look at them and begin to recognize them.

Consider center locations when organizing your room. A poor center plan shows no rhyme or reason for toy storage and no thought given to where art and messy projects will be done in relationship to cleanup. Children tend to play with toys where they are stored. If blocks are stored with housekeeping items and trucks in the dress-up area, then play will be disrupted and cleanup will be a disaster.

Classroom Designs and Decorations (cont.)

Sample Plans

Here are two sample plans for your classroom design. Remember, just as no two snowflakes are alike, there are no two classrooms alike. Your personality and allotted space will account for these differences.

The key word to a great classroom is functionality. While preparing your layout, keep in mind how well it will function for all your needs. Use the sample plan here and on the next page to help inspire your own ideas.

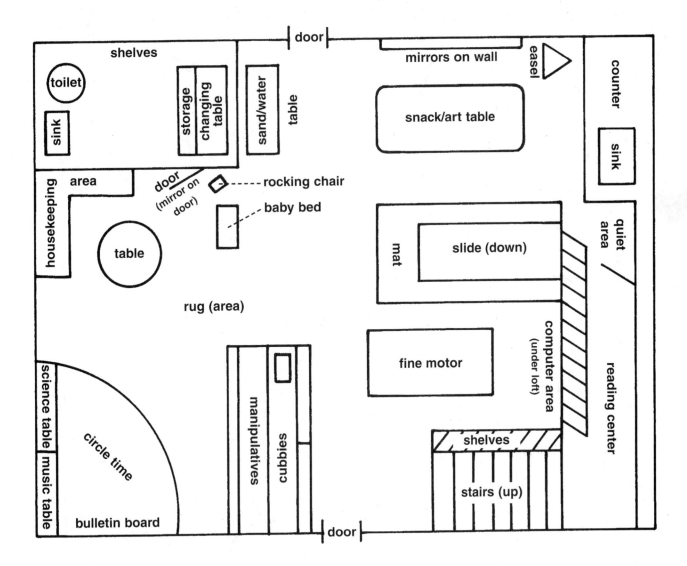

Classroom Designs and Decorations (cont.)

Sample Plans (cont.)

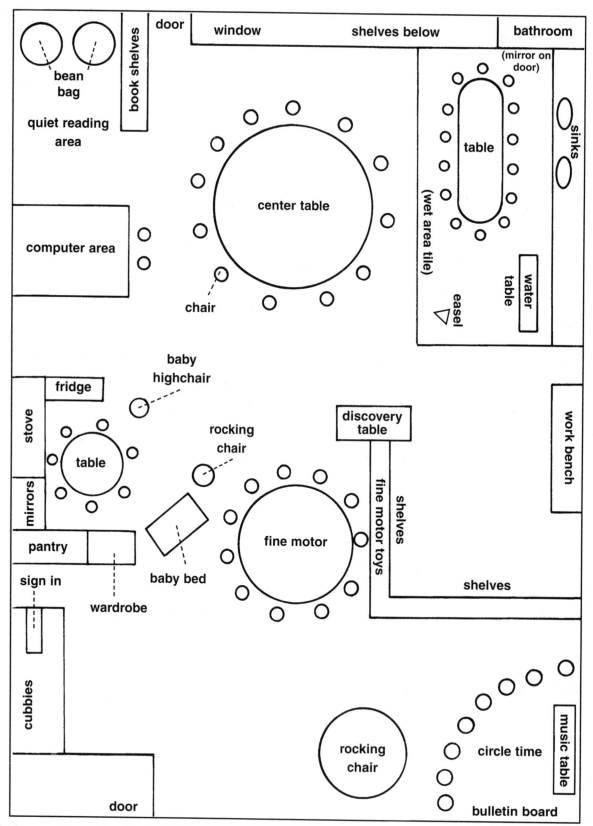

Classroom Safety Checklist

Providing a safe environment for children is the preschool teacher's first responsibility. Use this checklist to set up your room with safety in mind.

❏ Emergency (fire, earthquake, storm, etc.) plans are posted next to every doorway, clearly marking all exits.

❏ Entrances and exits are not blocked by furniture.

❏ Doors open and close slowly so no one will be bumped or get fingers and toes caught.

❏ Room is arranged to eliminate hard-to-supervise blind spots.

❏ Traffic areas are clear and free of objects to prevent tripping accidents.

❏ Tall cubbies and shelves are placed securely against walls or bolted down for stability.

❏ Furniture is positioned away from windows and high shelves to protect children who may climb on it.

❏ Furniture and cabinet corners are rounded or covered with foam molding to avoid injuries. Wood furniture is free of splinters.

❏ Carpet is tacked down so children and staff members will not slip or stumble.

❏ Unused electrical outlets are covered with safety caps.

❏ Appliances and electrical cords are kept out of children's reach.

❏ Cords for blinds are tied and placed out of children's reach.

❏ Low cabinet doors and drawers are equipped with safety latches.

❏ Cleaning materials and poisonous substances are kept in locked places inaccessible to children.

❏ First-aid supplies are stored in special containers out of children's reach. They are checked regularly and replenished.

❏ All plants are nonpoisonous and are placed in unbreakable containers.

❏ The hot-water temperature from faucets is not warmer than 110 degrees Fahrenheit (43 degrees Celsius).

Classroom Safety Checklist (cont.)

❏ Pet cages are kept clean, and the area around them is free of debris.

❏ Pet food is stored in secure containers out of children's reach.

❏ Small sharp objects such as safety pins, staples, thumbtacks, paper clips, and hairpins are not found in areas accessible to children.

❏ Sharp objects such as adult-sized scissors and knives are stored securely out of children's reach.

❏ Toys are larger than 1.25 inches (3.2 cm) in diameter so they cannot be swallowed or caught in a child's throat.

❏ Toys and equipment are in good repair with no splinters, sharp edges, chipped paint, or toxic finishes. All small parts are securely attached.

❏ Staff purses and personal belongings are kept out of children's reach.

❏ Hot beverages are consumed away from children and kept out of their reach.

To ensure the best safety possible in your classroom and school, rely upon the following resources:

- Your local licensing or public school regulations

- The NAEYC Position Statement on Licensing and Regulation of Early Childhood Programs in Centers and Family Day Care

  NAEYC
  1834 Connecticut Ave. N.W.
  Washington, D.C. 20009
  (800) 424-2460

- Caring for Our Children: National Health and Safety Performance Standards; American Public Health Association (APHA) and the American Academy of Pediatrics (AAP) (202) 789-5636

Checklist for Classroom Centers

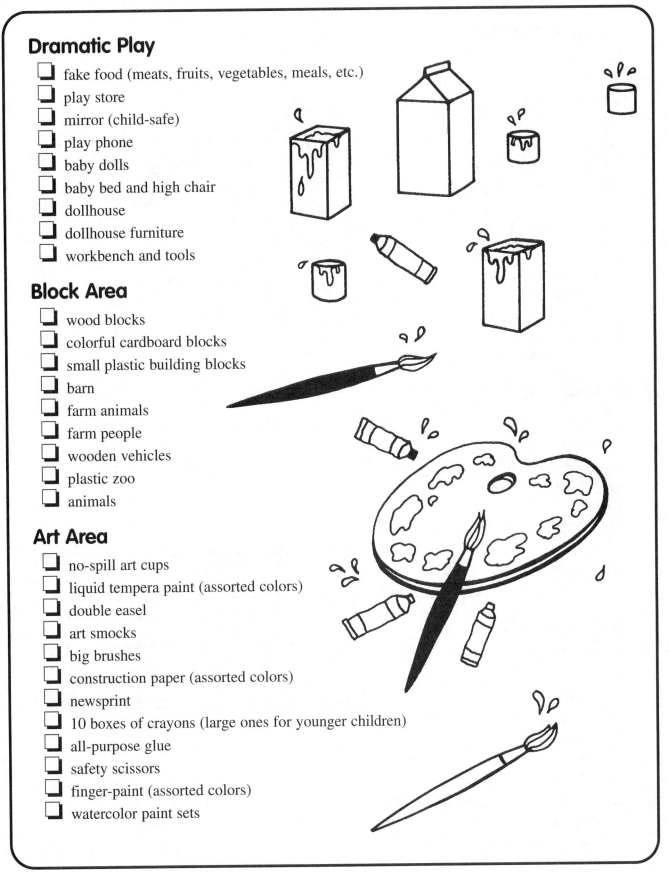

Dramatic Play

- ❑ fake food (meats, fruits, vegetables, meals, etc.)
- ❑ play store
- ❑ mirror (child-safe)
- ❑ play phone
- ❑ baby dolls
- ❑ baby bed and high chair
- ❑ dollhouse
- ❑ dollhouse furniture
- ❑ workbench and tools

Block Area

- ❑ wood blocks
- ❑ colorful cardboard blocks
- ❑ small plastic building blocks
- ❑ barn
- ❑ farm animals
- ❑ farm people
- ❑ wooden vehicles
- ❑ plastic zoo
- ❑ animals

Art Area

- ❑ no-spill art cups
- ❑ liquid tempera paint (assorted colors)
- ❑ double easel
- ❑ art smocks
- ❑ big brushes
- ❑ construction paper (assorted colors)
- ❑ newsprint
- ❑ 10 boxes of crayons (large ones for younger children)
- ❑ all-purpose glue
- ❑ safety scissors
- ❑ finger-paint (assorted colors)
- ❑ watercolor paint sets

Checklist for Classroom Centers (cont.)

Manipulative Play

- ❏ nesting cups
- ❏ flexible blocks
- ❏ bristle blocks
- ❏ tangrams
- ❏ puzzles
- ❏ sized cylinder blocks
- ❏ shape sorters
- ❏ floor puzzles
- ❏ attribute blocks and cards
- ❏ pegs and peg boards
- ❏ perceptual tracking toys
- ❏ sorting trays and objects
- ❏ beads and strings
- ❏ lacing cards and laces
- ❏ counters and trays

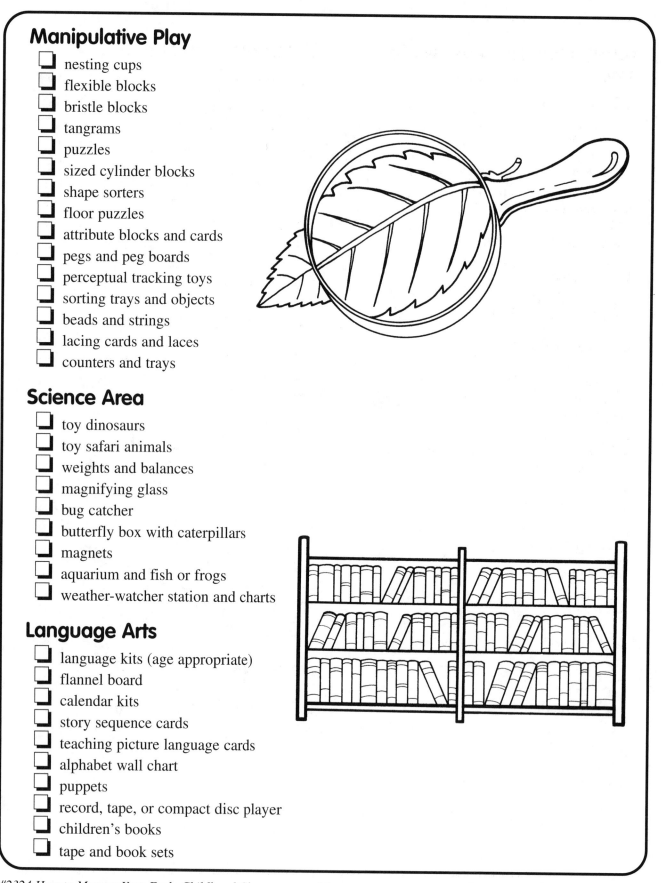

Science Area

- ❏ toy dinosaurs
- ❏ toy safari animals
- ❏ weights and balances
- ❏ magnifying glass
- ❏ bug catcher
- ❏ butterfly box with caterpillars
- ❏ magnets
- ❏ aquarium and fish or frogs
- ❏ weather-watcher station and charts

Language Arts

- ❏ language kits (age appropriate)
- ❏ flannel board
- ❏ calendar kits
- ❏ story sequence cards
- ❏ teaching picture language cards
- ❏ alphabet wall chart
- ❏ puppets
- ❏ record, tape, or compact disc player
- ❏ children's books
- ❏ tape and book sets

Checklist for Classroom Centers (cont.)

Indoor/Outdoor Gross Motor Area

❏ 14-inch (35 cm) tricycles

❏ wagons

❏ activity gyms (age appropriate)

❏ crawl-through tunnel

❏ swing

❏ hammock swing

❏ mats to go under all swinging toys

❏ balance beam

❏ mats to surround balance beam

❏ scooter board

❏ rock-a-boat (when turned over, these are steps)

❏ playground balls

❏ tennis balls

❏ large wall mirror for indoor play

❏ plastic bat and ball

❏ mini-trampoline with handles

❏ ball pit and balls

❏ sand and water table with lid

❏ sand toys

❏ basketball hoop and balls

Classroom Furniture

❏ moveable audio center

❏ cubby cabinet

❏ see-through storage

❏ cabinet with storage bins

❏ adult rocking chair

❏ rectangular table

❏ round table

❏ kidney-shaped table

❏ child-sized chairs (at least one per student)

❏ cots (one per student)

❏ bulletin board

❏ chalkboard

❏ trash cans with lids

❏ stepstool

❏ toaster oven

❏ small refrigerator

❏ bookcase

❏ large carpet

❏ beanbag chairs

❏ large pillows

Cleaning the Classroom

A clean classroom makes everyone happy. Here are a few tips to share with your co-workers. It is up to the teacher to delegate who does what. If you are fortunate, you will have a cleaning staff to do some of the work. Take charge! (Daily and weekly cleaning checklists can be found on pages 20 and 21.)

Daily Cleaning

- Clean carpets and vacuum. Sometimes playdough and paint or some other substances need to be scraped or loosened before vacuuming.

- Sweep bare floors and wash them with a disinfectant (ammonia or germicide work well). (Dirty water should be dumped into the toilet and never into the sink.)

- Clean bathrooms by disinfecting the floor, changing table, sink, and the toilet inside and out.

- Discard soiled diapers from the diaper pail into dumpster. Replace trashcan liners.

- Clean sinks, countertops, cabinets, walls, doors, and doorknobs.

- Clean all windows and mirrors.

- Clean all tables and chairs with disinfectant.

- Bag and discard the trash in an outside dumpster.

- Take all dishes to the kitchen and wash them thoroughly.

- Spray a disinfectant on the toys, shelves, chairs, doors, and doorknobs.

- Wash countertop, cabinets, walls, and sinks of kitchen with ammonia or disinfectant.

- Unplug all coffeepots and appliances each night.

- Check for all lights (except security lights) to be turned off at the end of the day.

Weekly Cleaning

- Move the furniture in the classroom to check for things that may have fallen behind them.

- Clean and organize the toy shelves. Check for toys that need washing, fixing, or are broken and need to be thrown out.

- Clean out the refrigerator.

Notes:

- The "recipe" for a good disinfectant is one gallon (2 L) water to two tablespoons (30 mL) bleach. Put in a spray bottle and store out of the children's reach, preferably in another room.

- Sponges harbor millions of germs. Use disposable towels when possible and disinfect sponges after wiping up snack spills.

Center Signs

Housekeeping

Manipulatives

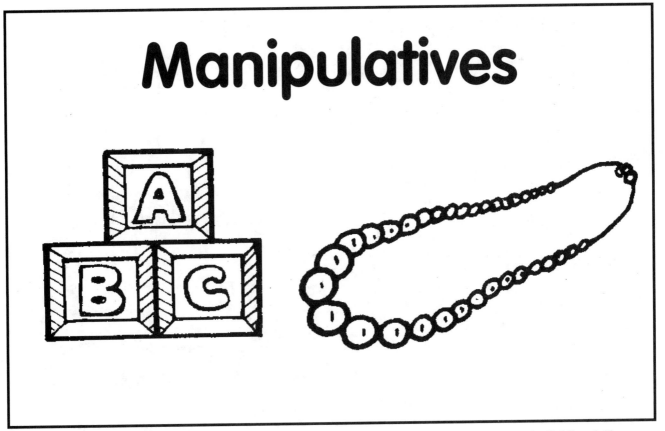

Center Signs (cont.)

Computer

Center Signs (cont.)

Science

Library

Daily Cleaning Tasks

Use this form to check off what needs to be done on a daily basis in your classroom.

Today's Date _____

_____ Straighten shelves.

_____ Clean pet cage if necessary.

_____ Water plants.

_____ Vacuum floors.

_____ Sweep bare floors.

_____ Wash floors with disinfectant.

_____ Disinfect toilet.

_____ Disinfect changing table or area.

_____ Clean sink.

_____ Discard soiled diapers into dumpster and replace trash can liners.

_____ Clean sink and countertop.

_____ Wipe cabinets, walls, doors, and doorknobs.

_____ Clean mirrors and windows.

_____ Clean tables and chairs with disinfectant.

_____ Bag trash and take it to the outside dumpster.

_____ Take all dirty dishes to the kitchen and wash them thoroughly.

_____ Wash countertop, cabinets, walls, and sinks of kitchen with ammonia or disinfectant.

_____ Spray a disinfectant on toys, shelves, doors, and doorknobs in the classroom.

_____ Refill paper products.

_____ Refill plastic glove supply.

_____ Fill cubbies with papers and art that is to be sent home.

_____ Unplug all coffeepots and appliances.

_____ Turn off the lights.

Weekly Cleaning Tasks

Use this form to check off what needs to be done on a weekly basis in your classroom and school.

Date _____

_____ Move furniture to check for things that have fallen behind shelves, sofas, etc.

_____ Clean and organize the toy shelves.

_____ Check for toys that need washing or repairs. Discard irreparable toys.

_____ Vacuum under toys and shelves.

_____ Refill the first-aid box.

_____ Thoroughly wash cabinets, walls, sinks, and floors with ammonia or disinfectant.

_____ Empty and clean the refrigerator.

_____ Check all cabinet locks to be sure they are secure.

Classroom Rules

1. Treat others as you want to be treated.

2. Be kind.

3. Use kind words.

4. Share with one another.

5. Take turns.

More Ideas

There are many ideas in this section of the book, and they are sure to inspire ideas of your own. Use this form to jot down your notes and the good ideas you hear from your colleagues.

My Ideas for the Classroom

Any teacher can have a neat desk. All that's needed is patience, organization, and about twenty-five drawers.

—*Claudia Lesman Boysen*

Make-It-Yourself Materials

This section of the book is filled with recipes for generic classroom materials you can make cheaply and easily.

Doughs for Creative Play

Cooked Dough

Ingredients:

- 1 cup (240 mL) flour
- $\frac{1}{2}$ cup (120 mL) salt
- 1 tablespoon (15 mL) cooking oil
- 2 teaspoons (10 mL) cream of tarter
- food coloring (optional)

Directions: Mix and heat until ingredients form a ball. Add a touch of food coloring if desired. Store in a sealed, air-tight container.

No-Cook Dough

Ingredients:

- 2 cups (480 mL) self-rising flour
- 2 tablespoons (30 mL) alum
- 2 tablespoons (30 mL) cooking oil
- 2 tablespoons (30 mL) salt
- $1\frac{1}{4}$ cups (300 mL) boiling water
- food coloring (optional)

Directions: Mix and knead, adding food coloring if desired. Store in a sealed, air-tight container.

Goopy Dough

Ingredients:

- $1\frac{1}{2}$ cups (540 mL) flour
- $\frac{1}{2}$ cup (120 mL) salt
- 1 tablespoon (15 mL) alum
- 2 cups (480 mL) boiling water
- $2\frac{1}{2}$ tablespoons (37 mL) cooking oil
- wintergreen scent (optional)
- food coloring (optional)

Directions: Mix and knead, adding food coloring and scent if desired. Store in a sealed, air-tight container.

Make-It-Yourself Materials (cont.)

Doughs for Creative Play (cont.)

No-Fail Dough

Ingredients:

- 1$\frac{1}{2}$ cup (360 mL) flour
- $\frac{3}{4}$ cup (180 mL) salt
- 1$\frac{1}{2}$ cup (360 mL) water
- 1$\frac{1}{2}$ tablespoon (22 mL) cooking oil
- food coloring (optional)

Directions: Sift dry ingredients. Mix liquids and add coloring if desired. Pour dry ingredients into liquid mixture. Cook over low to moderate heat, stirring constantly, until thickened mixture begins to loosen from sides of the pan. Knead. Cool. Store in a plastic bag or air-tight container. This dough does not need refrigeration.

Kool Dough

Ingredients:

- 2$\frac{1}{2}$ cups (600 mL) flour
- $\frac{1}{2}$ cup (120 mL) salt
- 2 packs unsweetened powdered drink mix
- 3 tablespoons (45 mL) cooking oil
- 2 cups (480 mL) boiling water

Directions: Mix dry ingredients by hand. Add oil and water. Stir quickly. When cooked, mix with hands. Store in a sealed, air-tight container.

Preschool Dough

Ingredients:

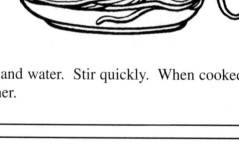

- 2 cups (480 mL) flour
- 2 cups (480 mL) water
- 1 tablespoons (15 mL) oil
- 1 cup (240 mL) salt
- 2 teaspoons (10 mL) cream of tartar
- food coloring (optional)

Directions: Mix all ingredients together in a saucepan. Cook and stir until mixture thickens and starts to stick to the pan. Knead out the lumps. Cool completely. Store tightly covered.

Make-It-Yourself Materials (cont.)

Doughs for Creative Play (cont.)

Shampoo Dough

Ingredients:

- $^3/_4$ cup (180 mL) flour
- $^1/_4$ cup (60 mL) thick shampoo
- $^1/_4$ cup (60 mL) white glue

Directions: Mix all ingredients together in a bowl. Knead until smooth. Add more flour if needed to create a workable consistency. Roll and cut into desired shapes. Let dry and paint.

Baker's Clay

Ingredients:

- 4 cups (960 mL) flour
- 1$^1/_2$ cups (360 mL) water
- 1 cup (240 mL) salt

Directions: Mix all ingredients together. Knead for six minutes. Add more flour if it the dough is sticky. Form shapes. Bake at 350 degrees Fahrenheit (180 degrees Celsius) for one hour.

Peanut Butter Dough

Ingredients:

- 1 cup (240 mL) smooth peanut butter
- 1 cup (240 mL) dried milk powder

Directions: Mix the peanut butter and milk together in a bowl. Use the dough on the same day it is made. Do not store for future use. (Note: This dough is edible!)

Make-It-Yourself Materials (cont.)

Doughs for Creative Play (cont.)

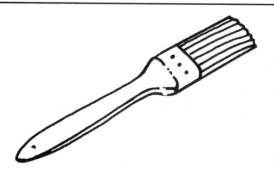

Skin Color Dough

Ingredients:

- 3 cups (720 mL) flour
- 1 cup (240 mL) salt
- 1 tablespoon (15 mL) oil
- 1 cup (240 mL) water
- various skin-toned tempera paints

Directions: Mix dry ingredients in a bowl. Mix with your choice of colors. Add oil to the water and gradually mix into dry ingredients. If it is too sticky, add flour. If it is dry, add water. Keep tightly covered when not in use.

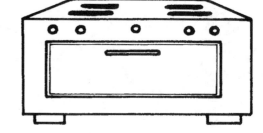

Baking Dough

Ingredients:

- 4 cups (960 mL) flour
- 1 cup (240 mL) iodized salt
- 1³/₄ cups (420 mL) warm water

Directions: Mix all ingredients in a bowl and knead for 10 minutes. Shape as desired. Bake at 300 degrees Fahrenheit (150 degrees Celsius) until hard or let air-dry for two to three days.

Mashed Potato Dough

Ingredients:

- 1 box instant mashed potatoes
- very hot water (Use with caution.)
- food coloring (optional)

Directions: Put instant mashed potatoes in a bowl. Gradually add water while stirring until the potatoes are stiff. Add food coloring for color variation.

Make-It-Yourself Materials (cont.)

Doughs for Creative Play (cont.)

Soap Dough

Ingredients:

- 2 cups (480 mL) soap flakes
- 2 tablespoons (30 mL) water
- food coloring (optional)

Directions: Pour soap flakes into a bowl. Add water gradually until the soap forms a ball when mixed with hands. Add food coloring, if desired. Form shapes and let dry. (This makes a great gift at holiday time.)

Paints

Salt Paint

Ingredients:

- $\frac{1}{8}$ cup (30 mL) liquid starch
- 2 squirts of food coloring
- paper plates
- $\frac{1}{8}$ cup (30 mL) water
- $\frac{1}{2}$ cup (120 ml) salt
- paintbrush

Directions: Mix starch, water, food coloring, and salt. Use the paint with a paintbrush. Keep stirring the mixture while you use it. As the paint dries, it will crystallize.

Tempera Salt Paint

Ingredients:

- 2 tablespoons (30 mL) salt
- 1 tablespoon (15 mL) water
- 1 tablespoon (15 mL) liquid starch
- few drops of liquid tempera paint

Directions: Mix all ingredients together in a small bowl. This is a roughly textured paint.

Make-It-Yourself Materials (cont.)

Paints (cont.)

Finger Paint I

Ingredients:

- 3 cups (720 mL) liquid starch
- $\frac{1}{2}$ cup (120 mL) water
- powdered tempera (enough to create the shade you want)

Directions: Mix all ingredients. Store in a closed container.

Finger Paint II

Ingredients:

- 3 cups (720 mL) liquid starch
- 1 cup (240 mL) soap flakes
- $\frac{1}{4}$ cup (60 mL) water
- powdered tempera paint

Directions: Mix all ingredients except paint in a pan on the stove. Boil to dissolve. When cool, add tempera paint. Stir. Store in a covered container.

Finger Paint III

Ingredients:

- 2 cups (480 mL) liquid starch
- 2 cups (480 mL) water
- 2 cups (480 mL) soap flakes
- 6 cups (1.5 L) hot water
- powdered tempera paint

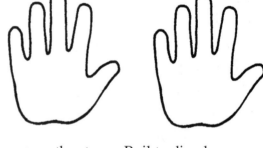

Directions: Mix and stir starch and cold water to a paste. Add hot water and cook until thick, stirring constantly. Add soap and tempera paint, stirring until the texture is smooth.

Make-It-Yourself Materials (cont.)

Paints (cont.)

Soap Paint

Ingredients:

- 3 cups (720 mL) soap flakes
- $^1/_2$ cups (360 mL) hot water

Directions: Mix ingredients in a plastic bowl. Whip with an eggbeater until stiff. Do not store this paint—make and use it as needed. Also, do not use soap powder since it will not stiffen.

Sensory Experiences

Bubbles

Ingredients:

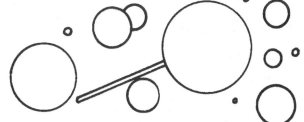

- 2 cups (480 mL) dishwashing liquid
- 6 cups (1.5 L) water
- $^3/_4$ cup (180 mL) white corn syrup

Directions: Combine the ingredients, shake in a sealed container, and let settle for four hours. Store in a covered container in the refrigerator. Allow to warm before use. Children under four years of age require supervision while using the bubbles. (While this formula is non-toxic, soap is an eye irritant.) Note that sunlight weakens the suds, so use in the shade or a protected area.

Oobeleegook

Ingredients:

- cornstarch
- water

Directions: Put cornstarch in a bowl. Add a little water at a time and let the children mix the ingredients with their hands. The mixture is hard when squeezed but will run through fingers like liquid.

Make-It-Yourself Materials (cont.)

Sensory Experiences (cont.)

Sludge Mud

Ingredients:

- 1 roll of toilet tissue
- 1 cup (240 mL) soap flakes
- 1 tablespoon (15 mL) Borax®
- water

Directions: Rip toilet tissue into small pieces and place in a bowl. Add the rest of the ingredients and mix well. This will create a slippery, slushy, muddy compound, enough for one child.

Creamy Finger Paint

Ingredients:

- shaving or whipping cream
- food coloring

Directions: Place whipping or shaving cream on a cookie sheet or directly on a table for a large play surface. (Whipping cream is best used on the cookie sheet.) Add colors as desired by the children. Surprisingly, cleanup is easy.

Activities for Make-It-Yourself Materials

Dough Activities

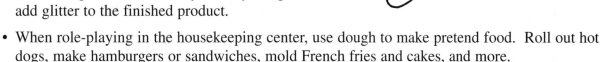

- Dough activities are physically worthwhile for young children. There is a vast array of things they can do with dough. Most toddlers need to strengthen their hands and finger dexterity. What a wonderfully fun way to build motor skills.

- When doing a unit on colors, make up a batch of dough that will last for the entire length of the unit. Seal it in a plastic bag or container. Each morning when the children come into the class, there is a ready-made, enjoyable activity that fits into your weekly theme just waiting for them.

- To add a special touch to any holiday dough, add glitter to the finished product.

- When role-playing in the housekeeping center, use dough to make pretend food. Roll out hot dogs, make hamburgers or sandwiches, mold French fries and cakes, and more.

- Free-play centers with playdough are very enjoyable for the children. Let the students pull, pat, roll, smash, grab, poke, and design whatever their hearts desire. Just set up the center with the dough on a table and a chair for each student plus one for the teacher. Once sitting at the center with the dough, it will not take long before the table is full of "dough" friends.

Paint Activities

- Soap and salt paints are great for winter art projects since the paints can give the illusion of snow and winter sparkle.

- Using soap and salt paint on dark paper creates a very dramatic look. Such dark paper is ideal for units on winter, black/white contrast, and hot and cold comparisons.

- The textures of soap and salt paints can be used for a sensory art project regardless of theme. The textures are very different from other paints and ideal for those who are sensitive to touch discernment.

- Remember, tempera paint can always be added to any homemade paint.

Activities for Make-It-Yourself Materials (cont.)

Sensory Experience Activities

- Bubble play is a great tool to elicit language from young children: "b-b-b-b-bubble," "more," "pop," "all gone," "big," and more.

- Getting a child's attention with bubbles is easy. Try this transition to a group activity: Sit in the place you would like the children to be and then get out the bubbles. The children will follow.

- Bubbles make a great reward for positive behavior. For example, if your goal is to get children to put something in a receptacle, blow the bubbles when they place the object inside. Only use the bubbles when they perform the desired objective.

- For all sensory recipes, remember the messier they are, the better to get the eyes, ears, nose, and of course the hands involved in experiencing the ooh and goo!

- The sludge mud recipe is great for tearing skills, a precursor to cutting with scissors.

- Add color to the sludge mud with tempera paint for units on colors, spring, farm animals (pigs love mud!), and any others that are appropriate.

- Use the creamy finger paint for mirror painting. To do so, spray shaving cream from the can onto a large mirror attached to the wall. Children can use their whole arms and fingers to write, smear, and pat the shaving cream. This also gives them an opportunity to look at themselves as they do this. Hint: Remove or cover their shirts prior to doing this activity.

- Place bubble wrap on the floor. Apply a large amount of the whipped cream or shaving cream to the bubble wrap and let them step, slide, and frolic in the creamy texture. Hint: Have the children wear bathing suits for this activity.

Teacher Desk Supplies

Here is a checklist of what every teacher should have available for a smoothly operating classroom.

- ❏ desk calendar
- ❏ plan book
- ❏ markers (permanent and drawing)
- ❏ crayons
- ❏ sticky notes
- ❏ black ink pens
- ❏ water or coffee mug
- ❏ paper clips
- ❏ masking tapes
- ❏ correction fluid
- ❏ bulletin board tacks
- ❏ stapler
- ❏ staples
- ❏ stackable letter trays
- ❏ notebook and binders
- ❏ teacher tote bag
- ❏ clipboard
- ❏ file drawer
- ❏ file folders
- ❏ apron
- ❏ Velcro®
- ❏ adult scissors
- ❏ camera
- ❏ film
- ❏ highlighter pens

Emergency Supplies

Here is a checklist of what every classroom should have in case of an emergency. The emergency bag should be located in an easily found spot. Keep it complete at all times. In case of power outage, field trips, fire, evacuation, or an environmental emergency, you will be prepared or ready to go. The other emergency supplies should be stored in an easily accessed cabinet.

For the Emergency Bag

- ❑ diapers or extra underwear for the children
- ❑ change of clothes (at least one set)
- ❑ emergency phone numbers, include one out-of-state contact per child
- ❑ sunscreen
- ❑ bug spray
- ❑ flashlight and fresh batteries
- ❑ pad of paper
- ❑ pen
- ❑ travel first-aid kit

For the Classroom

- ❑ first-aid kit
- ❑ bandages
- ❑ disposable rubber gloves
- ❑ thermometer
- ❑ change of clothes for each child
- ❑ water supply for three days
- ❑ nonperishable food supply for three days
- ❑ toilet tissue
- ❑ fire extinguisher
- ❑ flashlight and fresh batteries

Cleaning Supplies

This is a checklist of cleaning items for the classroom. Be especially conscious about where these items are located. They must always be stored in a locked cabinet out of the reach of children. This is preferably in a room the children never enter.

- ❏ bleach
- ❏ disinfectant
- ❏ plastic bags
- ❏ twist ties
- ❏ sponges
- ❏ mops
- ❏ bucket
- ❏ rubber gloves
- ❏ broom
- ❏ vacuum
- ❏ hooks
- ❏ paper towels
- ❏ several large bath towels
- ❏ several washcloths
- ❏ air freshener
- ❏ antibacterial dish detergent
- ❏ dishwasher, if possible

Working with Teaching Assistants

Sometimes a teacher enjoys the luxury of having a teaching assistant assigned to his or her room. If you are so lucky, approach the experience with a positive attitude. Above all, remember always to be kind and speak to your assistant as your equal. To maintain a positive working relationship, schedule time each week to review the matters of the week as well as any observations or concerns regarding the children. Open, honest communication between the two of you is key.

Here is a detailed job description for you and your assistant to review at the beginning of the school year. Be sure to provide the assistant with a copy of both pages. (Complete the "Additional Notes" sections as needed. Fill in the "Other Things" section with information specific to your school such as security procedures and codes, evacuation routes, release policies, and so forth.)

Morning Tasks

- Arrive on time and check the sign-in sheet to be sure the correct date is on it.
- Unlock the doors and turn on the lights.
- Offer a snack to all children who arrive before 8:00 A.M.
- When you are with the children, your responsibility is to them. Preparation of the room must wait until there is another adult to care for the children.
- Read to the children, interact with them, and keep them occupied.
- No breaks should be taken during this time.
- Whatever toys are used are to be put away in their places when no longer in use.
- Keep items available to children should they ask to use them (such as crayons, markers, paper, etc.).

Additional Notes:

_____

_____

Preparing the Room

- Check to be sure there is toilet paper, paper towels, gloves, and soap in the room.
- Pour the juice for the morning snack, prepare the snack, and check for all snack supplies.
- Wipe doorjambs and counters and clean the bathroom sink area.
- This is a good time to sanitize the toys or do teacher preparation for your teacher. Take the initiative—there is always something to do. A clean and tidy room is a reflection on you and your teacher!

Additional Notes:

_____

_____

Working with Teaching Assistants (cont.)

Outdoor Time

- Moving eyes and moving feet are essential here! Position yourself so that you can view all of the children. Try to space yourself so that there is at least one adult on each side of the playground. Always keep in mind that you are responsible for all of the children in your care when outdoors.
- In case of emergency or accident, act quickly and calmly.
- This is your time to interact with the children. Everyone should be active and busy. This is not a time to visit with other adults who may be outdoors.
- Have the children help you to tidy the playground when they are finished playing. This is a good way to get them to sort and categorize items (e.g., put all the tricycles together).

Inside the Classroom

- Follow the lead of the teacher. Do not talk to the children unless it is part of the lesson.
- Use positive reinforcement for good behavior and redirection when inappropriate behavior occurs. Avoid using the word "no." Always speak to the children in a positive manner. A smile goes a long way.
- Always look for the child who is not engaged in play. Your job would be to interact with that child and engage him or her.
- If you believe a child is sick, notify the teacher who will take the appropriate steps in managing the health of that child.
- Always be honest with the teacher. If you have a problem or see one that has risen in the classroom, express yourself. Open communication makes the best working situation.

Additional Notes:

_____

_____

_____

Other Things to Know About the Classroom and School:

_____

_____

_____

Working with Volunteers

What a treat it is to have adult volunteers to help with the operation of classroom activities and events. Here is a letter that you can use when you have a volunteer coming to your school. On the next page is a sheet of tips you can display or hand out as necessary.

Dear _____,

Thank you for volunteering your help on _____. We look forward to seeing you at _____ on that date.

For your information, here are some of the expectations we have for our volunteers:

- to help teachers move the children to and from the rooms or activities

- to assist the children in completing their tasks, but letting them do as much as possible by themselves

- to encourage interaction among the children and to interact with the children yourself

- to reinforce appropriate behavior with praise and attention*

- to talk with the children about colors, shapes, sizes, concepts such as "under" and "over," sensory words such as "hot" and "cold," and the names of things in general

- to use eye contact with the children

- to avoid speaking in "baby talk"

- to help the children to pay attention, to keep hands to themselves, to follow directions, and to take turns

- to model the actions to songs and fingerplays

- to assist the teacher or assistant by cleaning up messy art areas, after snack time, and during clean-up time.

If you have questions about what to do, just ask the teacher for advice or direction. Our goal is that each child leaves school each day with the experience of success.

We look forward to working with you throughout the year.

Thank you,

_____

*If an inappropriate behavior occurs, try to redirect the child to another activity or ignore the behavior as long as no one is getting hurt. Consult the teacher if you have a concern.

Tips for Assistants and Volunteers

- Interaction with the children is the best way to learn. Instead of standing back and observing, move in and talk with the children.

- State suggestions or directions in a positive manner rather than a negative one.

- Avoid trying to change behavior by methods which may lead to the loss of self-respect such as shaming or labeling the behavior as naughty or selfish.

- When a child talks to you, make a definite response. If you are busy, tell him, "I will talk to you in a minute," or redirect him to another adult.

- Use a natural voice, not a singsong one or baby talk.

- Speak slowly and distinctly.

- Avoid using too many words or giving too many directions at one time.

- Have a happy face and a pleasant voice. Enjoy the children and they will respond in that manner to you.

- Be kind and firm when redirecting an inappropriate behavior.

- Do not be afraid to interact with the children or to help when you believe your help is needed.

- Avoid making art models for children to copy.

- Remember, the important thing is the process children go through to create their art and their play, not the completed products.

- Do not be upset if a child does not respond to your approach. Discuss this with the teacher.

- If you are unsure about something, please ask us. We all learn through questions.

Volunteer Information Sheet

Name_____

Telephone number_____

Address *(including zip)*_____

Social Security number_____

Driver License number _____

State in which license was issued_____

How did you learn about our center? _____

_____

_____

Why would you like to volunteer? _____

_____

_____

Are you interested in volunteering on a regular basis or on an "as needed" basis? _____

Which days of the week are you available to volunteer? *(Please circle.)*

     Monday   Tuesday   Wednesday   Thursday   Friday

What hours are you available? _____

How many total hours are you interested in volunteering? _____

Are you currently employed? _____

Please list any previous employment experiences or volunteer experiences that would enhance your volunteer work at our center. Use the back of this paper, if necessary.

Please list your hobbies or talents. _____

_____

What types of volunteer work are you interested in doing? (Please circle.)

- assisting in the classroom
- clerical work
- running errands for office clerks
- maintenance
- cleaning
- other _____

Please list two references we may call on your behalf. _____

Name:_____ Phone: _____

Name:_____ Phone: _____

This center may require a background check as well as having your fingerprints on file. Do you agree to this?_____

Use these questionnaires with your families. This information is helpful to you to become better acquainted with the child.

Parent Questionnaire

Please complete this survey and return the form to school. The information will help us to become better acquainted with your child. Feel free to use additional paper as necessary. We would like to thank you in advance for providing this useful information.

1. By what name do you usually call your child? _____
2. Does your child have any disabilities including allergies that we should be aware of? If so, please explain._____
3. What terminology does your child use regarding the use of the bathroom? _____
4. If your child has attended preschool before, was the experience enjoyable? _____
5. Does your child have tantrums? _____
6. Does your child suck his/her thumb? _____
7. If your child has unusual fears, what are they?_____
8. Does your child use the following at home? *(Please circle.)*
   crayons   scissors   pencil   chalk   markers
9. What foods does your child like? _____
10. What foods does your child dislike? _____
11. List the names and ages of other children in your family.
    _____   _____   _____
    _____   _____   _____
12. What do you see as your child's strengths? _____
13. Is there any area in which you anticipate difficulty for your child? (e.g., sharing, following directions, etc.)_____
14. What goals do you have for your child? _____
15. What other information would you like us to know about your child? _____

Thank you for taking the time to fill out this questionnaire.

Child's name _____
Parent/Guardian Signature _____

Sincerely,

_____

More Ideas

There are many ideas in this section of the book, and they are sure to inspire ideas of your own. Use this form to jot down your notes and the useful ideas you hear from your colleagues.

Useful Teacher Tips

We need four hugs a day for survival. We need eight hugs a day for maintenance. We need twelve hugs a day for growth.

—*Virginia Satir*

First Things First

When parents entrust their children to early childhood educators, they do so with a portion of faith. They want to be assured that should their child need anything, including a hug or a bandage, the teachers will be able to supply it. In this section, you will find a variety of information concerning all the "bandages" teachers use for the many kinds of bumps and bruises that go hand-in-hand with being a child.

The forms found in this chapter are for your use. Copy and use them as needed. Please remember to check with your local health authority for specific rules and regulations that may relate to your specific area.

The best preparation for good health and safety is being aware of your full support system should an emergency arise. Complete the card below with the telephone numbers in your area. Display it in clear sight near your school telephone(s) for quick reference.

Fire Department _____

Police Department _____

Rescue Squad _____

Poison Control Center _____

Hospital _____

Emergency _____

About Medications

It is very important to have a record of what medications a child is taking, the dosage, and how many times in the day the medicine is to be given. All medication must be in prescription bottles with the labels well marked. It is best to have a physician's approval on file at the school. This should be on a form with the parent's signature and a place to put the time, date, and amount given, to be initialed by the person who administers the medicine.

It is also important to keep a sheet where the parent can communicate the last time his or her child received the medicine before coming to school. It is a good idea to have a medicine clipboard or notebook that can be easily taken from one area to another and made accessible to the parent to add special notes and instructions for the teacher/staff. A clipboard that can be moved from room to room and placed on a hook works well.

Also, remember that if for any reason 911 is called, the emergency operators will need all information regarding any medication the child has received. A medicine clipboard makes this information readily available.

As a rule, keep child emergency forms and the medicine clipboard or notebook near the telephone for quick reference. Also, keep posted important emergency numbers such as those for poison control, the fire department, and the police department. The best place for these numbers is near all telephones. (See page 46 for an emergency number card.) Also post a picture reference showing what to do for a choking infant, child, and adult.

Sample medicine forms can be found on pages 61–62.

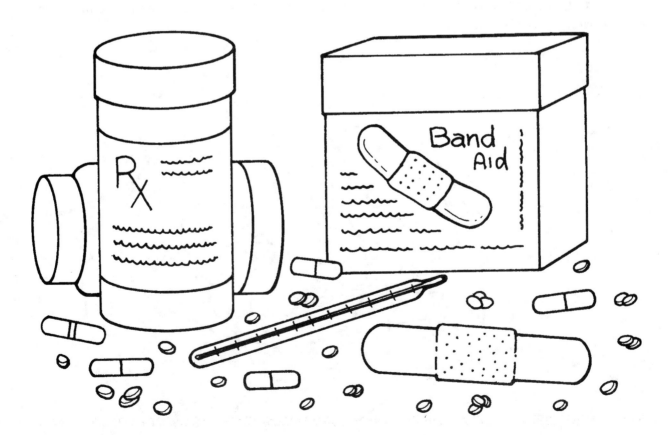

Duplicate this form to give to all parents.

Health Standards

Your child's health is a matter of major importance to all of us. To that end, all children attending this school should be free of contagious diseases, and all immunization records are to be in good standing. Children who have a fever, cough, or infection (throat, ear, eye, etc.) should not be brought to school. The staff will take the temperature of any child who seems ill during the school day. Any child running a significant temperature will be sent home in order not to infect other children, and any child showing obvious signs of illness will not be allowed in school.

Please keep your child at home if . . .

- he/she has begun taking antibiotics in the last twelve (12) hours.

- he/she has a constant cough.

- he/she has symptoms of a possible communicable disease (such as sniffles, reddened eyes, sore throat, headache, abdominal pain, and fever).

- he/she has a rash or has had diarrhea or vomiting during the previous twelve (12) hour period.

When a child has been absent due to illness, he/she should not return to school until he/she has been without a fever for at least twenty-four (24) hours.

Please notify the school office if your child does have a communicable disease so that we may inform the other parents. Thank you.

Sincerely,

_____

Child Emergency Information

Child's (preferred) name _____

Home address _____

_____

Home phone _____   Birthdate _____

Mother's name _____   Work phone _____

Mother's pager or cellular phone number _____

Father's name _____   Work phone _____

Father's pager or cellular phone number _____

Emergency contact _____   Phone _____

Child's Doctor _____   Phone _____

Child Emergency Information _____

Additional pertinent information (allergies, toileting skills, medications, etc.)_____

_____

_____

_____

Child's (preferred) name _____

Home address _____

_____

Home phone _____   Birthdate _____

Mother's name _____   Work phone _____

Mother's pager or cellular phone number _____

Father's name _____   Work phone _____

Father's pager or cellular phone number _____

Emergency contact _____   Phone _____

Child's Doctor _____   Phone _____

Child Emergency Information _____

Additional pertinent information (allergies, toileting skills, medications, etc.)_____

_____

_____

_____

To Be Posted

There is a variety of important information that should be posted in a prominent place in your school or classroom at all times.

- Fire Department phone number

- Police or Sheriff Department phone number

- Rescue Squad phone number

- Poison Control Center phone number

- Hospital (closest to center) phone number

- Children's allergies

- Names of children currently taking medicine along with medications, amounts, and times

- Children's names and birthdates

- School address and phone number

- Diagram of the evacuation plan and route to use in case of emergency

Note: At most Red Cross offices you can get posters that show what to do if a child is choking and how to administer cardiopulmonary resuscitation (CPR) if a child stops breathing. These should also be posted in a visible spot in the room.

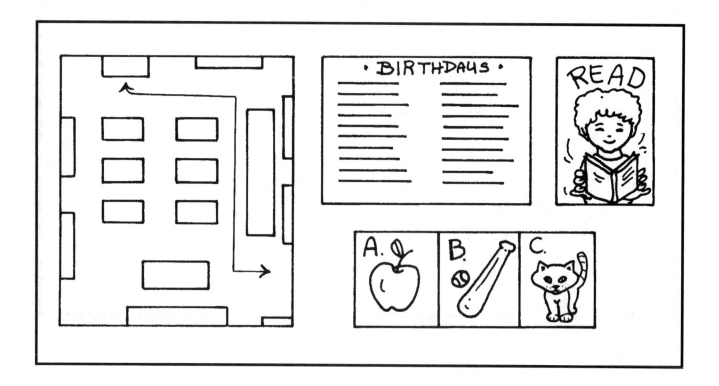

Accident/Incident Report

Child's name _____

Date and time _____

Type of accident or incident _____

_____

Name and address of center _____

_____

Report

Signature of person completing form _____

Parent/guardian signature_____ Date signed _____

Diaper Changing Procedure

Good sanitation practices are essential in regard to the diaper-changing area. Follow the guidelines below. Display the card at the bottom of the page for handy reference.

- Diaper changing surfaces should be clearly separated from all food-handling areas.

- Surfaces should be nonporous.

- Surfaces should be sanitized between uses.

- Diapering procedures should be followed consistently.

Diaper Changing Procedure

1. Put on disposable gloves, wipe the child clean, and put on a new diaper.

2. Wrap the used diaper and wet wipes with the diaper's self-stick tabs.

3. Put the used diaper in a plastic bag.

4. Discard the diaper in a plastic-lined container that is tightly covered.

5. Pull gloves off inside out and dispose in the container.

6. Disinfect the changing area after each use.

Infection Control Chart

To control the spread of infections, follow these guidelines closely. Keep this chart handy for easy reference.

- Prevent contact.
- Keep immunizations up to date.
- Stay home when sick.
- Isolate children who become sick.
- Notify parents about exposure to communicable diseases.
- Leave nonwashable toys at home.
- Turn away when someone coughs or sneezes.
- Do not share cups, bottles, plates, utensils, food, drinks, bedding, or mattresses.
- Do not kiss babies on the mouth.
- Do not use fingers as a pacifier.
- Discard unused refrigerated formula after twenty-four (24) hours.
- Change diapers away from food preparation areas.
- Dispose of trash daily.
- Do not touch blood.
- If blood is touched, wash hands immediately with antibacterial soap.
- Do not share toothbrushes, toothpaste, pierced earrings, nail clippers, or razors.
- Cover mouth when coughing or sneezing. (Although it is best to cough or sneeze into a disposable tissue and discard it immediately.)
- Cover unused food/formula and refrigerate.
- Cover sandboxes when not in use.
- Wear gloves when changing diapers.
- Fold soiled diapers inward and secure with tabs to contain urine and stool.
- Discard diapers, disposable soiled materials, and those used for cleaning in a tightly covered, foot-activated, plastic-lined container.
- Leave scabs alone.
- Cover cuts with bandages.
- Use barriers (gloves, tissues, towels) when caring for bloody injuries such as bleeding noses.
- Bag blood-soiled disposable items and discard in a tightly covered, foot-activated, plastic-lined container.
- Kill germs.
- Wash hands routinely.
- Wipe secretions, stool, and urine from the children's skin.
- Clean/disinfect contaminated surfaces, toys, toilet training equipment, food-preparation areas, sleeping materials, diaper-changing area, and bathroom areas.
- Wash soiled clothing and bedding.
- Follow routine housekeeping procedures.
- Apply disinfectant to cuts.
- Remove blood from surfaces, wash with a cleansing agent, rinse with a bleach solution (one part bleach to ten parts water), and air dry.
- Rinse blood-soiled clothing with cold water or hydrogen peroxide.

Hand-washing Procedure

The best way to prevent infection when working with young children is to kill and eliminate germs by hand washing. Post this hand washing procedure by all sink areas.

Hand washing

Why: Hand washing is the single-most important procedure for childcare providers in preventing the spread of infections to themselves, their families, their co-workers, and the children in their care. Teach children to do the same.

When: Wash hands . . .

. . . that are visibly contaminated or soiled.

. . . before eating, feeding, or giving a medicine.

. . . after using the toilet or changing a diaper.

. . . after drying tears, wiping noses, cleaning up vomit, or performing first aid.

. . . after caring for a sick child.

. . . after removing gloves.

How: For routine hand washing . . .

. . . wet hands.

. . . apply liquid soap.

. . . rub vigorously, lathering all surfaces for fifteen (15) seconds.

. . . rinse thoroughly under running water.

. . . dry completely with paper towels.

. . . turn off the faucet with the same toweling and discard.

Parent Notification of Contagious Disease

Date_____

Dear Parents:

This is to notify you that there has been a confirmed case of _____
in our center. Please look for these symptoms in your child:

Sincerely,

_____

First Aid Kit

A first-aid kit should be available in every classroom in the center. You can buy ready-made ones manufactured by the American Medical Association or make up your own kit.

Here is what you will need:

- ❏ first-aid guide
- ❏ gauze
- ❏ digital thermometer and probe covers
- ❏ instant cold compress
- ❏ triple antibiotic cream or ointment
- ❏ antiseptic cleaning wipes
- ❏ sterile pain-relieving gel
- ❏ tweezers
- ❏ tape
- ❏ eye pads
- ❏ sterile gauze pads
- ❏ plastic gloves
- ❏ blunt scissors
- ❏ bandages in assorted sizes for knuckles, fingers, and wounds of various sizes (extra long, medium, and small)
- ❏ Ace bandages
- ❏ paper
- ❏ pen
- ❏ sturdy case (for storage of all items)

A good resource book to have on hand in each classroom is *Baby and Child Emergency First Aid Handbook*, edited by Mitchell J. Einzig, M.D., Meadowbrook Press, New York, 1992. This book has illustrations, step-by-step instructions, and is easy to read and understand.

Providing a Safe Environment

Each state and local Health and Rehabilitative Services agency has determined what is to be used to provide the children with a safe and healthy environment. Check your local codes. Also, be sure that you are looking at the environment from a child's perspective. This should be kept in mind when purchasing toys or setting up the environment.

Here are a few things you may want to keep in mind when considering safety.

❑ Find out what disinfectant product is deemed safest to use for cleaning.

❑ Find out how much space is needed between each cot.

❑ Determine the room size and how many children are allowed in each room.

❑ Check on the size of toys and be sure they are not a choking hazard.

❑ See that there are no cords hanging from blinds that are accessible to children and could be a choking hazard.

❑ Check toys for rough edges or nails that can scratch or scrape a child.

❑ Check corners on furniture. If they have sharp corners, place tape over the corner to soften it should a child bump into it.

❑ Check to see that there is no chipped paint in the facility.

❑ Be sure that nontoxic paint has been used wherever children will be.

❑ Diapering areas require special precautions. Wearing gloves is necessary in some areas.

❑ Washing of hands prior to and after diapering children is a must.

❑ Latex gloves are used in many instances; however, some people are allergic to latex, and these allergies can be life threatening. It is best to use non-latex gloves if possible.

❑ Check to see if gloves are necessary when serving food, according to your local codes.

Health and Safety Documentation

Children

Each state and local health system agency has established what information is necessary to record regarding each child in every center prior to his/her entering the daycare or center. All immunizations must be up to date, and a copy of the child's birth certificate and a recent health examination must be noted. In many instances, if the family does not have a local physician, they may be able to obtain what is necessary at the local health department for little or no cost to them.

Each teacher and center coordinator should be aware of the documentation required for his or her particular setting. Files should be updated on a regular basis. Health departments can and do use surprise visits to check on these matters. The best advice is to be prepared.

On the pages in this section, you will find forms to help you document all matters of health and safety. These include Accident/Incident reports, Authorization for Medications, Child Emergency Information, Health Standards, and a daily note that you can send home to share what the child did at school on any given day.

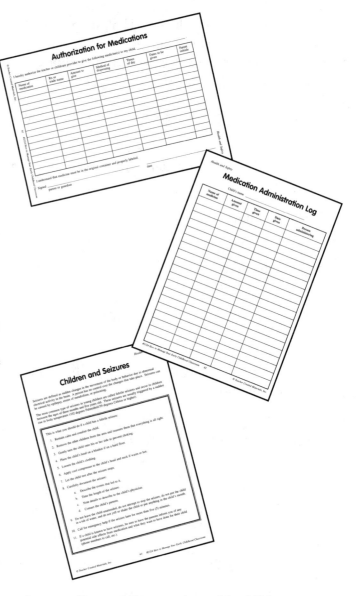

Employees

Each state and local system has requirements for employees. To work in a setting with children, a background check with fingerprints must be done and kept on file. Each employee should be certified in child and adult first aid, including cardiopulmonary resuscitation (CPR). Most states also have class requirements that must be met.

Please check to see what is necessary in your area. There are many requirements, and it is best to be clear on what is expected of you. For example, you may need to pass a test on items such as disposing of, or being exposed to, hazardous waste and blood-borne pathogens. Items such as this are not only necessary, but they are provided for your safety and the safety of those in your care.

Common Signs and Symptoms of Childhood Infection

Include this sheet with the other medical information in your classroom. Store it all in a handy location.

Coughing

May indicate respiratory infections such as bronchiolitis, sinusitis, viral pneumonia, influenza, parainfluenza, adenovirus, and pertussis.

Diarrhea

May indicate multiple infectious agents including salmonella, shigella, campylobactoer, rotavirus, enterovirus, and parasites.

Fever

A fever may be a general symptom of a viral or bacterial disease.

Headache

This may be a symptom of many illnesses. When accompanied by a fever, stiff neck, and sensitivity to light, it may indicate bacterial or viral meningitis.

Infected Skin or Sore

This may represent impetigo or wound infection. A child with an open infection such as this needs a doctor's note before being allowed in a day care setting where he or she might infect other children.

Irritability

Unusual irritability or unexplained crying should be reported to the child's parents or guardians. This accompanied with fever may represent viral or bacterial meningitis.

Itching on the Body or Scalp

Look closely for lesion or agents such as scabies and head lice.

Lethargy

This may be a general symptom of a virus or bacterial disease.

Pink Eye

Tearing, itching of the eye, swelling and tenderness, along with redness to the eye represent conjunctivitis, either viral or bacterial in nature.

Rapid or Altered Breathing

May indicate the respiratory infections listed above.

Rash

Generally a rash must be evaluated on a case-by-case basis. Whenever there is a question about etiology, a physician should be consulted.

Sore Throat

Respiratory infections, pharyngitis, tonsillitis, viruses, and group A streptococcus (strep throat) all may be indicated. Consult a physician.

Vomiting

This may be a general symptom of viral or bacterial disease.

Yellow Skin or Eyes

This may be a symptom of hepatitis, and the child should not be allowed in a day-care setting without the consent of a physician.

Recommendations for Exclusion from the Preschool Setting

To prevent spreading germs to other children and adults in the preschool, it is recommended that a child does not come to school sick. Below are some illnesses or conditions that would make it necessary for a child to stay home, as well as information regarding when it is appropriate to let the child return to school.

It is important to request the parents to notify the school when the child has a communicable disease so that other families can be informed. Use the form on page 55 for such notification.

Conditions, Signs, and Symptoms

Diarrhea: Look for an increased number of stools, increased amount of stool water, or decreased form that is not contained in the diaper or by toilet use.

Vomiting: Keep the child home if he or she vomits two or more times in the previous twenty-four (24) hour time span (unless the vomiting is determined to be due to a noncommunicable condition, and the child is not in danger of dehydration).

Mouth Sores: These are associated with the inability to control saliva. Keep the child home unless it is determined that the child is noninfectious.

Rash: The child must remain at home when the rash appears with a fever or behavior change. When it is determined to be noninfectious, the child may return to school.

Conjunctivitis: This appears as pink or red conjunctiva with white or yellow eye discharge, often with matted eyelids after sleep and eye pain or redness of the eyelids or surrounding skin. A physician's consent is required for readmission.

Tuberculosis: The child must be removed from the center until it is determined that he or she is non-infectious.

Streptococcal Pharyngitis: The child must be excluded for twenty-four (24) hours after treatment is initiated or when he/she is fever free for twenty-four (24) hours.

Head Lice: The child is excluded until the morning after the first treatment.

Scabies: The child is excluded until after treatment has been completed.

Varicella: The child is excluded until the sixth day after the onset of the rash or sooner if all the lesions have dried and crusted.

Pertussis: The child is excluded after the disease is confirmed by a laboratory, or if the disease is suspected based on symptoms or because coughing begins within fourteen (14) days of face-to-face contact with a person in the home or classroom who has a confirmed case of pertussis. The child may return to the classroom five (5) days after appropriate antibiotic therapy has been initiated.

Mumps: A child is excluded until nine (9) days after the onset of parotid swelling.

Hepatitis: This is a virus infection. A child is excluded until one (1) week after the onset of the illness and when jaundice, if present, has disappeared. The child may also return if passive immunoprophtkaxis has been administered to the appropriate children and staff.

Authorization for Medications

I hereby authorize the teacher or childcare provider to give the following medicine(s) to my child, _____ .

Name of medication	Rx or trade name	Amount to give	Method of dispensing	Times of day	Dates to be given	Parent initials

I understand that medicine must be in the original container and properly labeled.

Signed _____   _____
        parent or guardian   date

Medication Administration Log

Child's name _____

Name of medicine	Amount given	Time given	Date given	Person administering

Children and Seizures

Seizures are defined as sudden changes in the movement of the body or behavior due to abnormal electrical activity in the brain. A person has no control over the changes that take place. Seizures can be caused by epilepsy, errors of metabolism, or poisoning.

The most common type of seizures in young children are called febrile seizures and occur in children between the ages of three months and five years old. These seizures are usually triggered by a sudden rise in body temperature (102 degrees Fahrenheit/39 degrees Celsius or higher).

This is what you should do if a child has a febrile seizure:

1. Remain calm and comfort the child.

2. Remove the other children from the area and reassure them that everything is all right.

3. Gently turn the child onto his or her side to prevent choking.

4. Place the child's head on a blanket if on a hard floor.

5. Loosen the child's clothing.

6. Apply cool compresses to the child's head and neck if warm or hot.

7. Let the child rest after the seizure stops.

8. Carefully document the seizure:

    a. Describe the events that led to it.

    b. Time the length of the seizure.

    c. Note details to describe to the child's physician.

    d. Contact the child's parents.

9. Do not leave the child unattended, do not attempt to stop the seizure, do not put the child in a tub of water, and do not yell or shake the child or put anything in the child's mouth.

10. Call for emergency help if the seizure lasts for more than five (5) minutes.

11. If a child is known to have seizures, be sure to have the parents inform you of any potential side effects from medication and what they want to have done for their child (phone numbers to call, etc.).

Seizure Chart

Child's name _____

Parent instructions or comments (when to call 911, etc.) _____

_____

_____

Parent phone numbers (work/home)_____

Parent signature _____   Date _____

Date	Time	Duration	Comments	Contact person

More Ideas

There are many ideas in this section of the book, and they are sure to inspire ideas of your own. Use this form to jot down your notes and the helpful ideas you hear from your colleagues.

My Health and Safety Notes

We teachers can only help the work going on.

—*Maria Montessori*

The Natural Process of Early Childhood Development

The accompanying developmental checklists show skills for children eighteen months through five years of age. The skills are arranged in groupings of several months at a time and are meant to be used as a guide rather than as a rigid timetable. This information will help you to anticipate stages of normal child development in the areas of fine motor, gross motor, language, cognitive, self-help, and social skills. Each child will acquire these skills at his or her own pace. Some children develop them more quickly in one area and more slowly in another.

The toddler stage (eighteen months to three years old) is an exciting period of growth for children. They explore their environment using all five senses. They are the center of their universe, and the world revolves around them.

As children enter the "terrible twos," the experience does not have to become one of uncontrollable terror and mayhem. At this time, children are beginning to explore how much they can control their universe and what the limits are. The words "no" and "yes" become powerful ones, allowing them to take ownership of their own boundaries. With gentle guidance from parents and care providers, children can form limits of control that are compatible with the needs of others as well their own.

Learning for a toddler often occurs when an activity can be repeated over and over. For example, a toddler loves to dump things, put them back, and then do it again repeatedly. This simple activity is a challenge, and the child is striving to master it. There is delight in every accomplishment.

The preschooler (three, four, and five year olds) is becoming more autonomous. As he or she improves fine and gross motor skills, the child is able to meet many needs with little help from an adult. Dressing, undressing, using the bathroom, and eating are some activities a preschooler can now do independent from an adult.

Preschoolers spend most of their time playing. Play is very important to their development. Play offers an excellent opportunity for language development. They enjoy playing in groups of peers, participating in dramatic play, and having a chance to stretch their imaginations.

Of course, these are only guidelines. Every child has an individual pace and should not be compared to other children in general. Comparisons only become useful when a child's abilities are extremely disparate from others of his or her age. Further investigation into the cause of such variances may be worthwhile. Be aware of differences but do not jump to any conclusions. Most likely, any variance is perfectly normal.

Toddlers: 18 to 24 months

Child _____ Date(s)_____

Check all mastered skills.

Fine Motor

❏ Places six large round pegs into pegboard without help

❏ Imitates crayon stroke

❏ Strings one one-inch (2.5 cm) bead

❏ Claps hands

❏ Scoops with spoon or shovel

❏ Rolls a ball in imitation

❏ Folds paper

❏ Puts four rings on a peg

❏ Completes a three-piece formboard (circle, square, triangle)

❏ Inverts container spontaneously to obtain an object

❏ Throws a small ball

❏ Pounds, squeezes, or pulls off bits of clay

❏ Builds a four-piece cube tower

❏ Makes horizontal, vertical, and circular scribble after demonstration

Gross Motor

❏ Carries a large toy while walking

❏ Runs stiffly

❏ Walks backward

❏ Walks upstairs with one hand held by an adult (both feet on step)

❏ Sits in a small chair from a standing position by backing into it or sliding sideways

❏ Stands on one foot momentarily with assistance

Toddlers: 18 to 24 months (cont.)

Language: Receptive

❏ Understands most nouns

❏ Identifies three body parts by pointing and naming

❏ Follows a new instruction exactly. (Use object names a child knows but combine in a novel way; for example, "Put the doll on your head")

❏ Matches object to picture

❏ Matches sound to animal (picture or toy)

❏ Points to several clothing items upon request

❏ Understands personal pronouns, some action verbs, and adjectives

❏ Understands the concepts in, on, and under

❏ Matches sound to pictures of animals

❏ Understands "what" questions

❏ Follows three different one-step directions without gestures

Language: Expressive

❏ Says 15–20 different words spontaneously

❏ Asks for "more"

❏ Says, "All gone"

❏ Says own first name or nickname upon request

❏ Combines use of words and gestures to make wants known

❏ Names five other family members, including pets

❏ Names four toys

❏ Produces animal sound or uses sound for animal's name (i.e., cow is "moo-moo")

❏ Asks for some common food items by name when shown the item

❏ Asks questions by using a rising intonation at the end of the word or phrase

❏ Verb repertoire of common actions expands

❏ Begins to use "be" verb

❏ Begins to use past tense verbs

❏ Uses two-word sentences

❏ Uses intelligible words about sixty-five percent of the time

❏ Names two to three pictures spontaneously

❏ Imitates four word phrases

Toddlers: 18 to 24 months (cont.)

Cognition

- ❑ Purposefully explores environment
- ❑ Solves simple problems using tools
- ❑ Activates mechanical toy
- ❑ Rolls play dough and uses a brush with paint
- ❑ Explores cabinets and drawers
- ❑ Identifies personal property
- ❑ Matches object to like picture
- ❑ Matches sound to animal
- ❑ Remembers where objects belong
- ❑ Sorts like objects (e.g., pegs and cubes of same color)
- ❑ Identifies three body parts by pointing or naming
- ❑ Turns pages of a book one at time
- ❑ Begins to engage in symbolic play (e.g., uses stick for spoon)
- ❑ When playing, has inanimate objects perform actions (e.g., doll washes itself)

Self-Help

- ❑ Drinks from cup without assistance
- ❑ Eats meal by self with a spoon
- ❑ Chews most food well with rotary jaw movements
- ❑ Sucks liquid through a straw
- ❑ Distinguishes between edible and inedible objects
- ❑ Gives up bottle and pacifier completely
- ❑ Sits on potty chair with assistance
- ❑ Indicates need to use toilet (even if too late)
- ❑ Zips and unzips large, nonseparating zipper
- ❑ Removes coat that is not fastened
- ❑ Attempts to put on shoes
- ❑ Pulls down pants (elastic waist)
- ❑ Unsnaps front snaps
- ❑ Pulls up pants (elastic waist)
- ❑ Helps with handwashing
- ❑ Helps with drying hands
- ❑ Attempts to wash face
- ❑ Cooperates in toothbrushing
- ❑ Attempts to brush hair
- ❑ Cooperates with nose being wiped

Toddlers: 18 to 24 months (cont.)

Social

❑ Hands a book to an adult to read or to share

❑ Pulls another person to show him or her an action or object

❑ Says, "No, no," when near a forbidden object

❑ Shares object or food with one other child when requested

❑ Greets peers and adults when reminded

❑ Expresses affection physically and verbally

❑ Interacts with peers, using gestures

❑ Stays on task for three to five minutes

❑ Picks up toys and puts them away when requested

❑ Attempts to comfort others who are in distress

Observer _____

Additional comments:

Toddlers: 24 to 36 Months

Child _____ Date(s)_____

Check all mastered skills.

Fine Motor

❑ Holds crayon with thumb and finger

❑ Nests objects graduated in size

❑ Turns knobs

❑ Strings three to five one-inch (2.5 cm) beads

❑ Completes a three-to five-piece puzzle

❑ Unscrews a jar lid

❑ Holds scissors correctly

❑ Scribbles with a circular motion

❑ Aligns two or more cubes horizontally

❑ Hands work together in similar motion

❑ Hands work together in opposite motion

❑ Places tiny object in small container

❑ Draws a horizontal line, imitating an adult

❑ Draws a vertical line, imitating an adult

❑ Snips with scissors

❑ Builds a tower with six to eight cubes

❑ Points with his or her index finger

❑ Manipulates, pounds, and squeezes clay

❑ Manipulates hands and fingers in finger paint

❑ Strings five to ten half-inch (1.3 cm) beads

❑ Touches index finger with thumb

❑ Unwraps objects wrapped in paper (e.g., candy)

❑ Folds paper in half in imitation

❑ Rolls clay balls

❑ Takes apart and puts together snap toys

❑ Pounds pegs out of a work bench

❑ Draws circles, imitating an adult

❑ Makes first spontaneous designs

❑ Initiates three-block bridge, using cubes

❑ Builds an eight- to nineteen-cube tower

❑ Cuts five-inch (13 cm) paper in half

❑ Holds a pencil with thumb and fingers

❑ Aligns three cubes to make a train

Toddlers: 24 to 36 Months (cont.)

Gross Motor

- ❏ Moves up and down a small slide independently
- ❏ Stands on tiptoes for several seconds
- ❏ Jumps from bottom step to the floor
- ❏ Stands on one foot momentarily without assistance
- ❏ Walks upstairs, holding railing with both feet on each step
- ❏ Walks downstairs, holding railing with both feet on each step
- ❏ Jumps forward six to 18 inches (15–45 cm)
- ❏ Throws a playground ball five to seven feet (1.5–2.1 m)
- ❏ Balances on a balance beam momentarily with both feet
- ❏ Runs a distance of ten feet (3 m), avoiding obstacles
- ❏ Stands on one foot for one to five seconds without assistance
- ❏ Jumps backwards
- ❏ Walks upstairs, alternating feet while holding the railing
- ❏ Jumps over a small object
- ❏ Pedals a tricycle five to ten feet (1.5–3 m)
- ❏ Walks downstairs, alternating feet while holding the railing
- ❏ Catches a large ball with arms and body
- ❏ Climbs jungle gyms and ladders
- ❏ Walks backward ten feet (3 m)

Language: Expressive

- ❏ Sings phrases of songs
- ❏ Produces the following sounds clearly: p, b, m, k, g, w, h, n, t, d
- ❏ Uses three-word phrases
- ❏ Uses expressive vocabulary of 50 or more words
- ❏ Names five pictures
- ❏ Names eight common objects
- ❏ Imitates words spontaneously
- ❏ Uses past tense
- ❏ Uses size words (e.g., big, little)
- ❏ Refers to self, using pronouns
- ❏ Uses quantity words (e.g., more, some, all)
- ❏ Produces most sounds correctly at the beginning of words
- ❏ Replaces jargon with sentences
- ❏ Uses at least two prepositions (e.g., in, on, under, off)
- ❏ Uses –*ing* verb form (e.g., running)
- ❏ Converses in sentences

Toddlers: 24 to 36 Months (cont.)

Language: Expressive *(cont.)*

❑ Uses different semantic functions (nomination, possession, agent and action, action and object, recurrence).

Function	Visual cue	Verbal prompt	Possible correct response
nomination	child sees dog	What's that?	a doggie, that doggie, or see doggie
possession	picture of dog	What's this? Whose tail?	doggie tail
agent and action	toy car	What happened? What am I doing?	drive car, or car go
action and object	paper and pencil	What am I doing?	write paper, draw circle, or make something
recurrence	empty plate and picture of cake	What happened?	cake is gone, or need more cake

❑ Uses at least three different sentence types (declarative, imperative, negative, interrogative "yes/no," and interrogative "wh").

Type	Examples
Declarative	Me good boy. Daddy go bye-bye.
Imperative	You do it. Give cookie.
Negative	No do. Car no go.
Interrogative (yes/no)	Baby do? Dog bark?
Interrogative (wh)	What baby do? What's that?

❑ Vocalizes for all needs.

❑ Gives full name on request.

❑ Participates in storytelling.

❑ Recites a few nursery rhymes/songs.

❑ Repeats five-word sentences.

❑ Uses some irregular past tense forms consistently (e.g., went, did, was.)

❑ Controls voice volume 90 percent of the time.

❑ Uses *this* and *that* in phrases.

❑ Uses *is* in statements.

❑ Answers *who* questions with a name.

Toddlers: 24 to 36 Months (cont.)

Language: Receptive

- ❏ Points to five to seven pictures of familiar objects
- ❏ Understands the concept of *one*
- ❏ Selects pictures involving action words
- ❏ Matches identical simple pictures of objects
- ❏ Identifies six body parts verbally and/or with gestures
- ❏ Follows two-part directions
- ❏ Holds up fingers to tell age
- ❏ Understands basic categories (e.g., food, toys, animals)
- ❏ Understands category by function (e.g., eat, wear)
- ❏ Demonstrates beginning knowledge of size (e.g., big, little)
- ❏ Demonstrates beginning knowledge of place (e.g., front, top, back, up)
- ❏ Understands *where* questions
- ❏ Understands *yes* and *no*
- ❏ Begins to categorize by familiar function (e.g., shoe and sock)
- ❏ Matches three colors
- ❏ Carries out three simple, related commands given at once
- ❏ Matches similar pictures of objects
- ❏ Identifies objects by their function
- ❏ Matches basic shapes
- ❏ Matches geometric form with picture of shape
- ❏ Points to six body parts on a picture or doll
- ❏ Acts out verbs
- ❏ Associates body parts with their function
- ❏ Gives more than one object when asked in the plural form (e.g., blocks)
- ❏ Points to an object that "is not the same" as the other three objects
- ❏ Matches five colors
- ❏ Listens to stories
- ❏ Gives one item when asked for one, even when several are present
- ❏ Understands pronouns
- ❏ Demonstrates an understanding of three shapes

Toddlers: 24 to 36 Months (cont.)

Cognition

❑ Plays with water and sand

❑ Identifies several rooms in the house

❑ Demonstrates use of objects

❑ Demonstrates an awareness of classroom routine

❑ Identifies clothing items for different occasions

❑ Finds detail in a favorite picture book

❑ Recognizes familiar adult in a photograph

❑ Engages in simple make-believe activities

❑ Names six body parts

❑ Knows own sex and sex of others

❑ Acts out familiar actions (e.g., cooking, feeding baby)

❑ Matches objects that have the same function (e.g., brush and comb)

❑ Understands concept of *two*

❑ Counts to three

❑ Names one color

❑ Identifies several colors by pointing

❑ Gives correct age verbally or with gestures

❑ Looks at books independently and points to and comments on pictures

❑ Names a missing object when shown three objects, one is removed, and the child is asked which one is missing

❑ Identifies familiar objects by touch

❑ Stacks rings in correct order

❑ Sorts three colors by color

❑ Can sequence actions into a meaningful order (e.g., paste on brush, cap on tube, brush teeth)

❑ Understands *front* and *back*

❑ Understands *open* and *closed*

Toddlers: 24 to 36 Months (cont.)

Self-Help

❑ Holds fork in fist and attempts to use it

❑ Drinks from cup and replaces it on table without spilling

❑ Holds spoon in fingers with palm up

❑ Unwraps food (e.g., candy, banana, etc.)

❑ Scoops food with a fork

❑ Gets drink without assistance from drinking fountain

❑ Feeds self with a spoon without spilling

❑ Pours liquid into a glass without help, but with some spilling

❑ Keeps lips closed while chewing

❑ Wipes mouth with a napkin

❑ Swallows food in mouth before taking another bite

❑ Anticipates need to eliminate in time to avoid accidents

❑ Distinguishes between urination and bowel movements

❑ Uses toilet with assistance. (Has daytime control)

❑ Urinates by self in toilet

❑ Flushes toilet

❑ Removes shirt

❑ Puts on socks

❑ Undresses completely without assistance

❑ Puts on pants (does not need to fasten)

❑ Puts on shoes (does not need to be on correct feet or tied)

❑ Unbuttons two large buttons

❑ Knows front and back of coat

❑ Knows front and back of pants

❑ Puts on coat

❑ Puts on T-shirt

❑ Unbuttons small, front buttons

❑ Unzips separating, front zipper

❑ Unsnaps snaps

❑ Turns water on and off

❑ Washes hands using soap without assistance

❑ Washes face with assistance

❑ Dries hands without assistance

❑ Brushes teeth with assistance

❑ Wipes nose when requested to do so

Toddlers: 24 to 36 Months (cont.)

Social

- ❏ Chooses and plays with a toy independently
- ❏ Imitates household chores
- ❏ Engages in make-believe play
- ❏ Knows difference between boys and girls
- ❏ Plays with other children appropriately
- ❏ Cooperates with requests 50 percent of the time
- ❏ Brings object from another room when requested
- ❏ Says "please" and "thank you" when reminded
- ❏ Attempts to help with chores
- ❏ Takes part in a simple game with a peer
- ❏ Makes a choice when asked
- ❏ Begins to show patience
- ❏ Begins to understand simple rules
- ❏ Identifies own sex
- ❏ Shares toys with some prompting
- ❏ Plays dress-up
- ❏ Demonstrates an understanding of feelings
- ❏ Sings and dances to music
- ❏ Greets familiar people
- ❏ Participates in circle games
- ❏ Plays for 10 to 15 minutes with an activity of choice
- ❏ Avoids common dangers (e.g., broken glass and busy street)

Observer _____

Additional comments:

Preschoolers: 36 to 48 months

Child _____ Date(s)_____

Check all mastered skills.

Fine Motor

❏ Strings small beads

❏ Unscrews and screws a three-inch (7.5 cm) lid

❏ Makes first designs or spontaneous forms

❏ Puts tiny objects into small container

❏ Folds paper in half without a model

❏ Grasps pencil between thumb and forefinger (tripod grasp)

❏ Places six pegs in a pegboard

❏ Cuts dough or soft clay with a cookie cutter

❏ Imitates drawing a diagonal line

❏ Imitates drawing a cross

❏ Cuts five-inch (13 cm) paper in two

❏ Beginning to show hand preference

❏ Puts together a six-to eight-piece puzzle

❏ Winds up a wind-up toy

Gross Motor

❏ Walks upstairs, alternating feet without holding railing

❏ Broad jumps over string or object two inches (5 cm) high

❏ Hops on one foot one time

❏ Kicks a large ball that is rolling

❏ Kicks a stationary ball

❏ Walks on tiptoes 10 feet (3 m)

❏ Throws a playground ball underhand to an adult

❏ Rides tricycle independently around corners

❏ Jumps forward a distance of 10 inches (26 cm)

❏ Avoids obstacles in path while running

❏ Runs on toes

❏ Gallops forward 10 feet (3 m)

❏ Pushes and pulls a wagon

Preschoolers: 36 to 48 months (cont.)

Language: Receptive

- ❑ Demonstrates an understanding of basic categories (e.g., food, animals, family)
- ❑ Demonstrates an understanding of *yes/no* questions
- ❑ Demonstrates an understanding of *when* questions
- ❑ Understands pronouns
- ❑ Begins to understand time concepts (e.g., *now* and *today*)
- ❑ Demonstrates an increased understanding of adjectives
- ❑ Understands basic functions (e.g., what people eat and wear)
- ❑ Carries out requests involving prepositions
- ❑ Points to pictures depicting adjective qualities
- ❑ Points to or places objects *up* and *down*
- ❑ Carries out a series of two unrelated commands
- ❑ Points to 18 body parts
- ❑ Understands an increased number of pronouns
- ❑ Describes what will happen next

Language: Expressive

- ❑ Uses some classification names (e.g., food, toys)
- ❑ Says *can* and *will* occasionally
- ❑ Begins to show conceptual understanding of the future
- ❑ Answers *how* questions
- ❑ Use of the verb *to be* expands
- ❑ Uses the word *why* as an all-purpose question
- ❑ Tells about immediate experiences
- ❑ Talks on the telephone, waiting for his/her turn to respond
- ❑ Uses verbs with nouns
- ❑ Combines three words to make a three-word noun phrase
- ❑ Carries on a conversation
- ❑ Uses contractions
- ❑ Uses conjunctions in sentences
- ❑ Uses plurals
- ❑ Asks *why, what,* and *where* questions
- ❑ Tells how common objects are used
- ❑ Uses four-to five-word sentences

Preschoolers: 36 to 48 months (cont.)

Cognition

❑ Points to 18 body parts

❑ Names 15 body parts

❑ Matches 11 colors

❑ Points to seven colors

❑ Names three colors

❑ Matches circles, squares, and triangles

❑ Points to two shapes

❑ Counts three objects

❑ Counts to 10 in imitation

❑ Matches one-to-one correspondence (three or more objects)

❑ Understands the concept of *one more*

❑ Points to *long* and *short* objects

❑ Identifies objects as *hard* and *soft*

❑ Sorts by length, shape (three shapes), and size

❑ Identifies objects as *square* or *round*

❑ Puts together two parts to make a whole

❑ Understands *up* and *down*

❑ Matches sequence or pattern of blocks or beads (three to six)

❑ Understands *top* and *bottom*

❑ Sequences a three-part story correctly

❑ Understands *over* and *under*

❑ Identifies *boy* and *girl* on request

❑ Understands *next to* and *beside*

❑ Tells if an object is *heavy* or *light*

❑ Understands *slow* and *fast*

❑ Understands *empty* and *full*

❑ Tells which objects go together (e.g., sock and shoe, nail and hammer)

❑ Understands *in front* and *in back*

❑ Understands *tall* and *short*

❑ Understands *more* and *less*

❑ Names pictures as *same* and *different*

❑ Sorts pictures by classification (e.g., animals, toys, vehicles)

❑ Adds two parts to drawing of incomplete person

❑ Can answer comprehension question such as "What should you do when you are hungry?" or "What should you do when you are sleepy?"

❑ Demonstrates an understanding that different activities occur at different times of day

❑ Matches letters of the alphabet (uppercase to uppercase)

Preschoolers: 36 to 48 months (cont.)

Self-Help

❑ Feeds self entire meal when food is cut up

❑ Eats while holding fork in fist, some spilling

❑ Uses spoon without spilling

❑ Swallows food in mouth before taking another bite

❑ Cleans up spills

❑ Stay dry during naps

❑ Stays dry at night

❑ Males can urinate in toilet by standing

❑ Snaps front of clothing

❑ Can find own clothing and put it on

❑ Puts on own coat, jacket, or sweater

❑ Puts on underpants

❑ Unbuttons front buttons

❑ Pulls off front-opening clothing completely

❑ Pulls off pull-over clothing completely

❑ Puts on dress or shirt

❑ Unlaces shoes

❑ Completes total handwashing procedure

❑ Dries face independently

❑ Washes hands and face with soap when adult regulates water

❑ Brushes teeth with verbal instruction

❑ Puts comb/brush in hair

Preschoolers: 36 to 48 months (cont.)

Social

❏ Follows rules in group games led by adult

❏ Identifies self in mirror by name

❏ Attends to music or stories for 10 to 15 minutes

❏ Says "please" and "thank you" without reminders 50 percent of the time

❏ Attempts to help an adult with tasks by doing part of the chore

❏ Will share with others if a trade is involved

❏ Plays for 15 to 20 minutes with an activity of choice

❏ Separates easily from mother in familiar surroundings

❏ Answers telephone, calls to adult, or talks to familiar person

❏ Takes pride in own achievement

❏ Works in a small group at least 10 minutes

❏ Begins to play well with one or two children

❏ Takes turns with assistance

❏ Cooperative play begins to replace parallel play

❏ Uses blocks or other objects to build complex structures

❏ Plays dress-up in adult clothes

❏ Puts toys away neatly when asked

❏ Stays in outdoor play area

❏ Adapts to new tasks

❏ Shows increasing control over emotional reactions

Observer _____

Additional comments:

Preschoolers: 48 to 60 months

Child _____ Date(s)_____

Check all mastered skills.

Fine Motor

❏ Places small pegs in holes on board

❏ Traces letters

❏ Draws a recognizable picture

❏ Draws a person with a head and three clear features such as arms and legs

❏ Draws a square, imitating an adult

❏ Cuts a five-inch (13 cm) square within one-half inch (1.3 cm) accuracy

❏ Cuts a triangle with two-inch (5 cm) sides within one-half inch (1.3 cm) accuracy

❏ Puts paper clip on paper

❏ Creases paper with fingers

❏ Completes inset puzzles with five to ten pieces

❏ Prefers one hand most of the time

❏ Usually uses non-dominant hand

❏ Builds a five-block bridge through imitation

❏ Cuts pictures from a magazine

❏ Places key in lock and opens lock

❏ Writes a few identifiable letters/numerals and attempts first name

❏ Strings small beads, reproducing color and shape sequence

❏ Draws a line from one object to another

❏ Prints own first name with a model

❏ Builds structures with blocks or Tinker Toys

Gross Motor

❏ Attempts a somersault

❏ Runs around objects/corners without falling

❏ Rides a "two-wheeler" with training wheels

❏ Skips five to ten seconds

❏ Walks down stairs, alternating feet without holding the railing

❏ Jumps up eight to ten inches (20–26 cm)

❏ Hops on preferred foot for a distance of two feet (60 cm)

❏ Throws playground ball approximately twelve feet (3.6 m)

❏ Catches playground ball with both hands

❏ Throws small ball overhand 10–15 feet (3 m)

❏ Bounces ball two times and then catches it

Preschoolers: 48 to 60 months (cont.)

Gross Motor *(cont.)*

❑ Walks heel-toe for 10 feet (3 m)
❑ Walks on a low balance beam independently
❑ Jumps forward 10 times without falling
❑ Can do forward somersaults independently
❑ While swinging, pumps swing to sustain motion

Language: Receptive

❑ Carries out a series of three directions
❑ Understands *which* questions
❑ Can point out absurdities in pictures
❑ Understands *how many* questions
❑ Understands statements involving negations
❑ Demonstrates understanding of passive sentences (e.g., boy hit girl vs. girl hit boy)
❑ Understands time-related words such as *soon, later,* and *in a few minutes*
❑ Understands time-related words that occur within one to two days (e.g., not today, different day)
❑ Understands precise nouns within categories (e.g., shoe, slipper, boots)
❑ Understands abstract adjectives (e.g., ugly, pretty, wild, tame)
❑ Understands comparative adjective forms (e.g., big/bigger, short/shorter)
❑ Points to *same* and *different*
❑ Properly sequences a four-picture story

Language: Expressive

❑ Uses verb *to have* to form past tense
❑ Uses *could* and *would* in speech
❑ Communicates cause-and-effect relationships (e.g., is broken, does not work)
❑ Uses compound sentences (e.g., I hit the ball, and it went in the road)
❑ Rhymes simple words
❑ Uses relationship words (e.g., sister, brother, grandmother, and grandfather)
❑ Tells final word in opposites analogies
❑ Tells familiar story without pictures for cues
❑ Asks increasing number of questions for new information
❑ Pronouns are used consistently
❑ Shows shifting reference in conversation (e.g., I and you)
❑ Uses adjectives to describe and specify
❑ Uses all basic number words
❑ Uses determiners (e.g., *a* parade, *this* dog)
❑ Verb repertoire expands to senses (e.g., smell, taste, feel)
❑ Uses comparatives (e.g., big, bigger, biggest)

Preschoolers: 48 to 60 months (cont.)

Cognition

❑ Names 20 body parts

❑ Points to 11 colors upon request

❑ Names eight colors

❑ Matches five shapes

❑ Names *circle, square,* and *triangle*

❑ Counts by rote to 29

❑ Matches groups having an equal number of objects (1–10)

❑ Picks up specified number of objects on request (1–10)

❑ Counts 10 objects demonstrating one-to-one correspondence

❑ Understands *fat* and *skinny*

❑ Understands *long* and *short*

❑ Understands *thick* and *thin*

❑ Names *first, middle,* and *last* positions

❑ Understands *rough* and *smooth*

❑ Identifies an object that does not belong in a set

❑ Identifies a penny, nickel, and dime by pointing

❑ Recognizes a repeating pattern in a sequence and can continue it

❑ Recalls four objects seen in a picture

❑ Names or points to the missing part of a pictured object

❑ Tells color of named objects

❑ Identifies by name the numbers one through ten

❑ Identifies picture by the quality asked (e.g., what we carry when it is raining, what shines in the sky at night)

❑ Points to 20 upper case letters

❑ Points to 15 lowercase letters

❑ Tells what is missing when one out of three objects is removed

❑ Gives a reason why an object does not belong in a group

❑ Properly sequences a four-picture story

❑ Completes analogies (e.g., an apple is red, and a banana is _____)

❑ Names objects that perform familiar actions (e.g., something that flies)

❑ Points to or places an object *before* and *after*

❑ Points to or places an object *above* and *below*

❑ Points to or places an object *around* and *through*

❑ Points to or places an object *by, beside,* and *between*

❑ Understands time concepts such as *today, yesterday,* and *tomorrow*

❑ Recognizes own printed name

❑ Matches some words

❑ Recognizes some words

❑ Matches lowercase letters

Preschoolers: 48 to 60 months (cont.)

Self-Help

❏ Serves self at table

❏ Helps set table by correctly placing plates, napkins, and utensils with verbal cues

❏ Clears place at table

❏ Uses knife for spreading soft toppings

❏ Refills glass from pitcher with no spilling

❏ Cleans up spills, getting own cloth

❏ Uses correct utensils for food

❏ Eats different types of food

❏ Drinks from water fountain without aid of an adult

❏ Attempts cutting with a knife

❏ Uses bathroom independently. Goes to bathroom in time, undresses, wipes self, flushes toilet, and dresses unaided

❏ Adjusts clothes after going to toilet

❏ Remembers to wash/dry hands after using toilet

❏ Buckles and unbuckles belt or shoes

❏ Inserts belt in loops

❏ Buttons clothing independently

❏ Puts zipper foot in catch

❏ Selects appropriate clothing

❏ Knows when clothes are inside out and turns them if needed

❏ Hangs up clothes on a hanger

❏ Distinguishes front and back of clothing

❏ Puts shoes on correct feet

❏ Tightens shoelaces partially with a vertical pull

❏ Laces shoes

❏ Brushes/combs hair with or without assistance

❏ Wipes and blows nose 75 percent of the time without reminders

❏ Knows which faucet is hot and cold

❏ Washes hands and face with soap independently

❏ Brushes teeth alone

Preschoolers: 48 to 60 months (cont.)

Social

❑ Takes turns in play without adult supervision

❑ Performs simple errands

❑ Needs help beginning and stopping an activity

❑ Enjoys singing and dancing to music

❑ Asks for assistance when having difficulty

❑ Follows rules in group games

❑ Apologizes without a reminder 75 percent of the time

❑ Greets familiar adults without a reminder

❑ Cooperates with adult requests

❑ Tattles a great deal, exaggerates, and boasts

❑ Engages in socially-acceptable behavior in public

❑ Plays cooperatively with peers for extended periods without adult intervention

❑ Is social and talkative

❑ Spontaneously takes turns and shares

Observer _____

Additional comments:

Kindergarten Readiness Skills

Use this checklist to help determine kindergarten readiness. Children meeting seventy-five percent (75%) or more of the expectations will be determined to have met the expectations for school readiness.

Mark each blank with a "Y" for "yes," an "N" for "not observed," or "NA" if not applicable.

Name _____ Date _____

School District _____ School_____

Health and Physical Development

____ The child's immunizations are current.

____ The child displays physical development appropriate for kindergarten.

- throws and catches a large ball
- walks the length of the balance beam
- broad jumps with both feet
- runs without falling

Personal, Social and Behavior Development

____ The child complies with rules, limits, and routines.

____ The child engages successfully in kindergarten tasks.

- works successfully at center-time activities
- engages in math tubbing
- participates in calendar activities
- participates in class discussions

____ The child demonstrates appropriate interactions with adults.

- contributes to class stories or daily news
- understands that in school, children are expected to do what teachers ask

____ The child demonstrates appropriate interactions with peers.

- cooperates with others during center time activities
- takes part in playground activities and snack-time interactions
- exhibits patience in daily routine

____ The child copes effectively with challenges and frustration.

- copes with being away from parents or caregivers

____ The child demonstrates appropriate self-help skills.

- uses the bathroom independently
- washes and dries hands
- eats snacks neatly

____ The child expresses needs appropriately.

- asks for whatever help is needed

Kindergarten Readiness Skills (cont.)

Preacademic, Academic, and Literacy Development

____ The child demonstrates verbal communication skills necessary to succeed in kindergarten.
- understands questions and gives appropriate answers
- responds to stories
- participates in sharing-time activities

____ The child demonstrates problem-solving skills necessary to succeed in kindergarten.
- knows a few ways to try to settle arguments
- uses flexibility to choose another task when first choice is unavailable

____ The child follows verbal directions.

____ The child demonstrates curiosity, persistence, and exploratory behavior.

____ The child demonstrates an interest in books and other printed materials.

____ The child attends to stories.

____ The child participates in art and music activities.

If the child has received special education services, please respond to the following.

Does the child participate in Exceptional Student Education (ESE)?   **yes   no**

If yes, does the child receive services in a mainstreamed educational environment?   **yes   no**

Does the child require adaptive equipment, devices, and/or technologies to participate
in school?   **yes   no**

If yes, explain. _____

_____

_____

_____

_____

_____

_____

_____

Toddler's Creed

If I want it, it's mine.

If I give it to you and change my mind later, it's mine.

If I can take it away from you, it's mine.

If I had it a little while ago, it's mine.

If it's mine, it will never belong to anybody else, no matter what.

If we are building something together, all the pieces are mine.

If it looks just like mine, it is mine.

—Anonymous

A teacher affects eternity. He can never tell where his influence stops.

—*Henry Adams*

Curriculum Development

Curriculum for preschool children is not easily defined. The phrase most often heard in regard to preschool curriculum is "developmentally appropriate practices." Developmentally-appropriate practices are not a curriculum or method of teaching, but a way of thinking and working with young children. The curriculum is planned according to its suitability per age group, and it includes opportunities to meet the different needs, interests, and maturation levels of the children.

In developing a curriculum, be sure to pay attention to time, tasks, materials, and how the environment will be structured. Each area of the children's development is important. The children must be active participants, interacting with both adults and their peers. Also, the experiences must be meaningful and authentic to help them learn with the greatest success. Strive for intrinsic (internal) motivation rather than extrinsic ("I will receive something for doing this.").

There are three curriculum designs that are used by preschool teachers and centers. They are individual lessons, the unit approach, or a combination of the two.

As a teacher plans for large group, small group, and individual learning, the plans should center around the children's interests and the materials to be used. Also take into consideration the important skills to be developed in the children: creative representation, language and literacy, initiative and social relations, movements, music, classification, seriation, number concepts, space, and time.

Individual lessons refer to planning lessons for the needs of a single child. For example, imagine that Susie has a weak pincer grasp and poor writing/coloring skill. You may decide to create a lesson of dropping clothespins in a bottle or can to work on her eye-hand coordination and grasp. Other students may also play along and enjoy the game; however, your motivation for planning was solely related to Susie's need.

A unit approach to lesson planning uses a theme as the central feature of a lesson. For example, imagine that you decide to teach a unit on pets. First you must decide what you want the children to know about pets. For language/cognition skills you may want them to identify the pets by name as well as the sounds they make. Your art projects may involve creating cat and dog puppets from paper bags. When the puppets are dry, you can use them to pretend, talking like cats and dogs. At circle time, your puppet can ask important skill questions of the children (such as naming objects or telling about the weather). At the end of circle time, the children can walk like a cat to the snack table. In this way, every area of your curriculum is designed around the theme you have chosen.

It does not have to take weeks to plan a thematic unit. The unit can be as long as or as short as you believe it will take to master the skills you want the children to learn.

Curriculum Development (cont.)

To develop a curriculum, here are some important steps to follow:

- Assess what the child's entry behaviors and skills are.
- Determine what the child will learn in the developmental areas by the end of the year (long term goals).
- Determine what skills the child needs in order to accomplish the long-term goals. (These are called short-term goals.)
- Determine the order of the short-term goals (easiest to most difficult).
- Gather the materials.
- Determine how you will know when the child has met the short-term goals.
- Teach your unit.
- Evaluate how successful the activities/unit were for you and the children.
- Proceed or revise the plans based on what skills are still needed or learned.

Children develop concepts about themselves, others, and the world around them by observing, interacting with others, and looking for ways to solve a problem. They need to have daily opportunities to do the following:

- develop large and small muscles through their play activities.
- develop language skills through stories, poems, dramatic play, talking, and drawing.
- express themselves through art and music.

As you keep these daily goals in mind, be sure to include varied cultural and non-stereotyped experience in your activities. In creating your daily plans, be sure to provide a balance of rest, quiet activities, and active movement throughout the day. A good rule of thumb is the "up-down-up" method of planning. This reminds you to plan activities that alternate between "up and moving" and "low and quiet" learning activities. For example:

Sample Unit: farm animals

Monday: cow

Group *(down):* Identify the cow, say the cow sound, count cows, talk about cows, identify the cow that is first and last, identify big cows, identify small cows, explain where we find cows, and tell what products come from cows.

Music *(up):* Sing "Old Mac Donald Had a Farm." Pretend to be cows, mooing around the room.

Art *(down):* Paint with colored milk or tear brown paper and glue it on a cow shape.

All the areas addressed in this developmentally-appropriate curriculum are wrapped into the farm animals theme. In fact, so much can be done with "cows" alone that it could be a theme for a few days or an entire week. (Remember, it is important to adjust your curriculum to the age group you are teaching. You will develop a sense for when you have taught the unit long enough. You will also have the pleasure of watching the children begin to use what you teach them in their creative free play throughout the day.)

The Eight Intelligences

Children learn in a variety of ways. Most educators agree that there are eight identifiable intelligences through which children learn. Most children and adults have one or two that are their strongest modes of learning. As educators, it is important to structure teaching methods to include all eight intelligences so that each child can learn according to his or her strengths.

Here is a list of the eight intelligences and how they apply to curriculum and children's learning. (The sequence of the list does not indicate any priority or sense of importance.)

1. **Verbal/Linguistic:** The children think in words and enjoy stories, reading, writing, creative activities, drama, and anything that involves words.

2. **Logical/Mathematical:** These children think logically. They like experiments, puzzles, sorting, collections, and figuring out things.

3. **Spatial:** These children like pictures. They enjoy art, drawing, and creatively using their imaginations.

4. **Bodily/Kinesthetic:** These children learn through movement and bodily sensation. They like to dance and move, to touch, to construct, and to role-play.

5. **Musical:** These children learn by melody and rhythm. They love to sing, hum, and listen. They have a good sense of beat and rhythm. They enjoy poetry.

6. **Interpersonal:** These children learn by communicating. They enjoy organizing, planning, relating to others, making friends, and group activities. They are very empathetic.

7. **Intrapersonal:** These children like to be alone. They daydream, meditate, plan, have personal hobbies, and seem to be very independent.

8. **Naturalistic:** These children love the out-of-doors. They have the ability to understand, relate to, and function in the natural world. They have a sense of awe and wonder about the world around them.

By using the sensory approach to teaching advocated in the introduction (page 4), a teacher can incorporate all sensory areas (sight, sound, taste, smell, and touch) into the activity plans. By using the eight intelligences and all sensory areas to meet the goals of the unit, the teacher is able to touch on the strengths of all the students while building up and stretching areas that are not quite as strong. All of these considerations are applied when creating a curriculum that is developmentally appropriate. What you have in the end is a successful program that is meeting the developmental needs of the preschoolers in your center. What you have is success!

The Whys of Lesson Planning

Circle Time: When a child participates in circle time, he or she learns to listen, to sit still, and to understand the spoken word. Children learn that their ideas have value to the other children in the group and to the teacher or adult in charge. Children learn to wait their turn when others are talking and to participate in turn taking. They learn new vocabulary words, memory skills, and sequencing skills when they sing songs, recite poems, and take part in fingerplays. Children learn names of others, and they learn to cooperate and be considerate of others.

Cooking: When a child participates in cooking projects, he or she learns about nutrition, tastes, and food groups. Children learn how hot and cold change things. They learn about whole-part relationships and the concepts of volume and measure. They become aware of other cultures and their foods. Their vocabulary improves. Children learn that when they do something, there can be an immediate reward, and it may taste good!

Playing Instruments: When children play with rhythm instruments, they learn the rhythms of music. They learn that language of *fast*, *slow*, *loud*, and *soft*. Playing with instruments helps children find another way to express themselves. Children learn listening skills, auditory discrimination, and how to interpret and understand signals and cues.

Singing: When children sing songs, they learn the principles of music and rhythm. They learn vocabulary, and they improve memory skills and sequencing skills. Auditory and phonics skills are polished. When singing songs, an awareness of other cultures can also be developed.

Dancing: When children dance, they learn balance and coordination. They become conscience of moods and rhythms of music and how to express themselves physically.

Reading: When children look at books and listen to stories, they learn that books are important and enjoyable. Reading is one of the most important indicators of future academic successes. That is why it is imperative not only to introduce the children to books and stories, but also to try to foster a love for them. Children learn that print is written-down words. They learn that they can express their own ideas in print and create their own books. They learn that pictures also tell stories and that they can express themselves in the same way. They exercise their imaginations by creating their own stories. They learn to recognize certain words in print, and they feel like a million dollars when they think they can read. When they recognize words in print, children begin to use more complex thought and language patterns. Children learn that they can follow the development of thoughts and ideas in the plot of a story.

The Whys of Lesson Planning (cont.)

Gluing: When children use paste and glue to create a collage, they exercise imagination and creativity. They develop the concepts of shape, size, location, and design. Children learn about different textures and how to create patterns and designs. Children also learn how to distinguish patterns from backgrounds. This is an important pre-reading skill.

Cutting: When children use scissors, they learn to control the small muscles in their hands. They exercise their imaginations and creativity. The concepts of shape, size, color, and location are also learned.

Painting: When children paint at an easel, they develop their imaginations and creativity, eye-hand coordination, relationships of space and size, and their understanding of the concepts of symmetry, balance, and design. Children feel that they can purposely create shapes, express their feelings and ideas, and that their ideas have value.

Finger-painting: When children finger-paint, they learn to exercise their creativity and imaginations and to develop their eye-hand coordination. Children learn about the concepts of *shape*, *size*, and *location*. They learn that colors mixed together make new colors. They learn also that this is an acceptable way to make a mess. It is highly enjoyable for the children to be together with friends making messes!

Drawing: When children scribble and draw, they learn how to hold a pencil or other drawing tool. They learn how to control the pressure on the drawing tool, and they improve eye-hand coordination. They exercise creativity and imagination. They learn about color, shape, size, and location. They learn that their ideas have value and that they can express themselves in drawing as well as in words when describing what they drew.

Clay Modeling: When children use dough or clay, they learn to see the shapes against the background of the table. They learn about shapes, sizes, length, and height. They see the negative space when cookie cutter shapes are taken away. Hand muscles are developed when the child squeezes and pounds the clay. Even science concepts are learned by playing with clay-like products. For example, children learn that the quantity of something remains even when the shape changes. The list of concepts learned is endless.

Toilet Training

Toilet training is an important part of your preschool program and an important step in the children's independence. There are two words that must be applied when considering toilet training for the children in your program: patience and consistency. You must have both, or toilet training will be the most difficult thing you do with the child throughout the entire year. Of course, it is also best to have the cooperation of the parents.

Here are a few prerequisite skills that you can use to decide whether the child is ready.

Does the child . . .

- understand simple directions?
- show pride in learning a new skill?
- show periods of strong independence?
- imitate adult behaviors like brushing hair and washing his/her own face?
- show interest in the toilet?
- sit quietly for short periods of time?
- stay dry for two hours at a time?
- show an awareness of having just urinated or having had a bowel movement?
- have good language skills to communicate the need "to go"?

If the child has shown most of these behaviors, he or she is ready to begin. Remember though, toilet training takes each child a different amount of time to achieve. It has to be a cooperative effort between the facilitator (you) and the child. You can not "make" a child use the toilet. They have the ultimate control of the system. You have the ultimate control of the situational setup.

Introducing the Potty Chair

Introduce the potty chair to the child and show how it is similar to the toilet. Let him or her sit on it fully dressed. Let the child sit with a book. Getting comfortable with the chair is the goal at this level. When selecting a potty chair, be sure the chair is stable and will not easily topple. The child needs to feel secure. If you use an adapted seat on the toilet itself, be sure there is a stepping stool handy so that the child can be independent in getting off the toilet as well. Getting their own stool for the potty is an activity that also creates a sense of pride in children. They can now be "big kids on the big toilet."

Watching for Signs

Begin to watch for signs that the child is aware he/she is about to urinate or to have a bowel movement. If your child shows this awareness, you are ready to begin bowel training. Beginning with bowel training is recommended because children have more time to anticipate that the bowel movement is going to occur than when he or she has to urinate. If the child is signaling that he or she is having a bowel movement (hiding behind a chair, face turning red when they are going), then calmly encourage the child to use the toilet. If the child is reluctant or resistant, do not argue. Simply wait until the next time. This is where patience becomes essential.

Toilet Training (cont.)

Patience

While you are bowel training, the child is likely to urinate on the potty at some time.

Gradually she/he will learn to connect the feeling of a full bladder, urination, and the puddle or wet pants that result. You can try to anticipate the child's need to urinate. For example, if the child wakes up dry from a nap, encourage him or her to use the potty, but do not insist. Tell the child to use the toilet when ready.

Reinforcements

When the child is successful on the potty, it is good to use reinforcement as a reward for the behavior. Many parents use a piece of candy. You may want to use a star chart that you have made especially for the child. When the child uses the toilet, give him or her the star or sticker to put on the chart and verbally praise the child. This also allows the child to reinforce his or her own behavior when putting on the sticker. As always, be an enthusiastic audience. Success at the potty should be cheered and widely admired.

Training Pants

When the child has been successful, decide with the parent when the child is ready to wear training pants and when diapers are to be eliminated all together. Traditional cotton training pants are heavy-duty and extra absorbent. These are pulled on and off by the wearer. This helps put more of the control in the toddler's hands and improves the odds of getting to the potty on time. Disposable training pants are a cross between diapers and traditional training pants. These are ideal for those toddlers who are about to embark on the toilet-training adventure. They look like and are worn like training pants, but they absorb like a diaper. When these pants are soiled, they are thrown away instead of laundered. When accidents are few and far between, then it is advisable to transition to the traditional pants. Keeping a child in disposable trainers makes completing the toilet training process take even longer.

Accidents

Accidents are an inevitable part of learning to use the potty. Whether they are occasional or frequent, the less said about them the better. Making a fuss about an accident will only promote resistance in toddlers. Punishment is certainly never warranted for a toilet-training accident. When an accident happens, reassure the toddler with comments like "that's okay" or "Oh, you had an accident. Next time let's try to get to the potty." Then you should clean up the messy pants together and comment on how nice it feels to be in clean, dry clothes. Humiliation of the child will never work, and it is inappropriate. Just as in your classroom, the goal is to make this a positive event.

Hygiene

The best way to teach good hygiene habits is to start from the beginning. After using the potty, whether successful or not, teach the child to wash his/her hands with soap. You may have to use a great deal of positive verbal reminders before the child gains independence in this area.

Naptime

Naptime is crucial for children who stay all day or come to the center in the before-care hours. Sleep not only helps children to regain some of the energy they have expended during the day, but it is also critical to a child's growth.

Naptime is best set to a child's schedule. Children generally need to eat lunch between 11:00 A.M. and noon. After a nutritious lunch and a chance to use the potty, children love to hear a story as they settle into their cots for their naps.

Children should have a cot or mat that is theirs exclusively. They should be allowed to bring their own blankets, sheets, or cuddly toys for naptime. This will help the child to relax and be able to sleep well during naptime.

Setting up cots or sleeping mats so that naptime is a quiet, peaceful time is essential. There should be enough space between children so that they cannot touch one another or any toys around the room. Lights should be dimmed and nightlights placed in the room so that you can see each child easily without turning on overhead lights. Soft music is recommended as a background noise.

Allow the children to place their shoes under their cots or next to their mats. Removing shoes also helps to calm the children. Furthermore, it is a physical sign that the time for resting is here.

If you have a child who is uneasy about sleeping away from home, you may need to physically reassure him/her. Rubbing the child's back or rocking in the rocking chair can do this. Be sure to provide the comfort the child needs. However, remember that the ultimate goal is to get the children to lie quietly alone on their mats. Do not reinforce your soothing efforts longer than required. Be sure to wean the children from your assistance. It is important that they sleep on their own. Learning to do so is a key skill for all growing children.

Use this form to keep track of who is staying for lunch and naptime.

Lunch and Nap List

Please note if your child will be staying in school today for lunch and/or nap. Write "B" in the lunch column if you brought a lunch from home.

Thank you.

Date	Class	Child's Name	Lunch	Nap

Useful Themes

Here are some ideas to help you plan what to teach.

Animals
- zoo
- farm
- pets
- dinosaurs
- woodland animals

On the Move
- space
- transportation
- ocean
- bugs
- wind
- cowboys

Sports
- baseball
- football
- basketball
- golf
- soccer
- tennis
- volleyball

Cross-cultural Holidays
- Kwanzaa
- Chinese New Year
- Cinco de Mayo
- Mardi Gras
- Festival of Lights
- Martin Luther King, Jr. Day
- Presidents' Day
- Rosh Hashanah
- St. Patrick's Day
- Valentines Day

Occupations
- nurse
- dentist
- farmer
- teacher
- office worker
- grocer
- mail carrier
- librarian
- baker
- carpenter
- doctor
- astronaut
- restaurant worker
- painter
- police officer

The World Around Us
- cans
- ice cubes
- shadows
- sponges
- sticky things
- magnets
- pockets
- pasta
- pizza
- bubbles

General Topics
- colors
- numbers
- shapes
- sounds
- weather
- feelings

An easy way to choose what to teach is to take the number of weeks in a month and pick one theme per week, touching on four areas. For example, choose one color, one number, one object, and one language concept. In this way, it is easy to plan for the month. (Keep in mind, however, that some themes may take more than one week.) Save your plans so that you can use the successful ones again next year.

Fill in the missing information on this form and send it to parents to keep them informed.

Parent Bulletin

Dear _____ ,

You can be proud of your child. _____

is currently working on _____

at school. You can help at home by _____

_____

_____

_____ .

If you have any questions or comments, please write them below and return this form to school, or feel free to call me.

Thank you very much for your help, time, and effort.

_____
teacher

_____
date

Class Book

A class book is a great way to build unity within the families in your classroom early in the school year. Follow these steps:

1. Send home each family's page (page 105) to complete. Ask the family to attach a picture to it.

2. When you receive the finished pages, laminate them.

3. Punch holes in the pages and place them alphabetically in a three-ring notebook.

4. Decorate the cover of the book to match the theme of your classroom. (For example, if you decorate with bears, you might put a bear on the front and title the book *Beary Good Friends*.) If your classroom does not have a theme, choose any design you like.

5. On the inside front cover, write a list of the children's names.

6. Use this list to keep track of the children who have brought the book home to share with their families. (Place a check next to the name when the book has been taken.)

7. Continue to send the book home until every family has had a chance to share it with their child. It is recommended that each family keep the book for two to three days only.

Class Book Family Page

Please affix a photo
here of your
child or family.

My name is _____ . I am _____ years old.

The people in my family are _____ .

My favorite color is _____ .

My favorite things to play with are _____ .

My favorite food is _____ .

My favorite song is _____ .

As a family we like to _____

_____

_____ together.

Use this form to keep parents informed about their child's school day.

My School Day

Child's name _____   Date_____

Arrival: _____   Departure: _____   Mood: _____

Free Choice Play	Group Activities

Art	Music	Outside Time

Diapering/Toileting Schedule

Comments

Teacher _____

Use this sheet for letters and news to parents.

Here's the News!

Date _____

Dear Families,

Sincerely,

_____

Newsletters

Newsletters are a good way to keep communication active between the parents and the center. Parents feel reassured when they know what lessons and activities are coming for their children. In this way, the parents are a part of the learning process in the school. Newsletters are the perfect way to keep them up-to-date.

You should always post a lesson plan or newsletter to document what you are teaching. Use the forms on pages 109–120 and refer to the sample below as you feel necessary.

Follow these guidelines in creating your newsletter. (Each area on the sample is marked with a letter corresponding to the list.)

A. *date*

B. *greeting (If you use the term "families," you will not offend any single parents, blended families, or custodial grandparents.)*

C. *introduction*

D. *dates to remember*

E. *topic activities*

F. *songs and fingerplay words*

A. September 8, 1998

B. Dear Families,

C. Hope all of you had a nice "long" weekend. It was nice to see three families at the first parent meeting on September 1st.

D. Be sure to keep your calendars handy. There are several important dates to remember.

We have a field trip planned for Monday, September 14th. We will be taking the bus to the Huntington Beach Library for a special "Toddler" storytime, and then we will be off to McDonald's for snacks and fun in the play area. We need to leave school no later than 9:15! We will return by 12:30. Parents are welcome to come along! (cost $1.00)

For the month of September we will focus on the letter sound of "A," the color "RED," and the shape of "CIRCLE," along with the number concept of "ONE." This week we will use APPLES to learn these concepts.

E. Some things we will do are to pick 1 apple, put 1 apple on a picture of 1 apple, identify the big/little red apple, match red objects to the color card red, put red circles on a tree, look through red cellophane, match the red apple to the red apple with 2 or 3 choices, and draw a red circle, etc . . .

F. RED APPLE

A little red apple
Hung high in a tree (point upward)
I looked up at it (look upward)
And it looked down at me (look down)
"Come down, please," I called
And what do you suppose—
That little red apple
Dropped right on my nose! (touch nose)

THE APPLE TREE

Away up high in an apple tree,
(point up)
One red apple(s) smiled at me.
(make one fist in air)
I shook that tree as hard as I could,
(pretend to shake tree)
Down came the apple (s)
And mmmm, were they good!
(rub tummy)
(Note: You can add two in place of one.)

September News

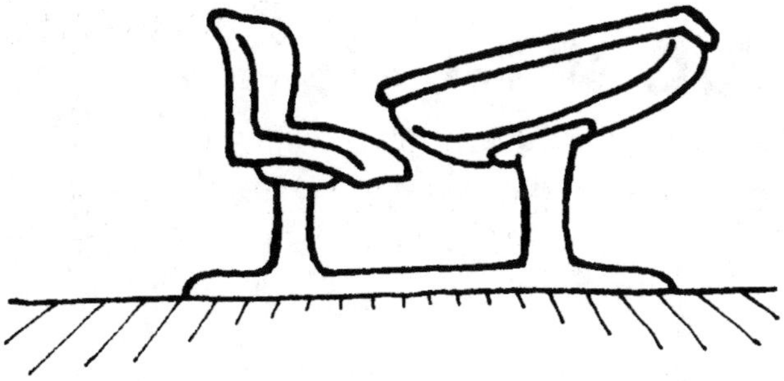

Date_____

Dear Families,

_____

_____

_____

_____

_____

_____

_____

_____

_____

_____

_____

_____

_____

_____

_____

_____

_____

_____

_____

_____

_____

_____

_____

_____

_____

October News

Date_____

Dear Families,

_____

_____

_____

_____

_____

_____

_____

_____

_____

_____

_____

_____

_____

_____

_____

_____

_____

_____

_____

_____

_____

                                       _____

                                       _____

November News

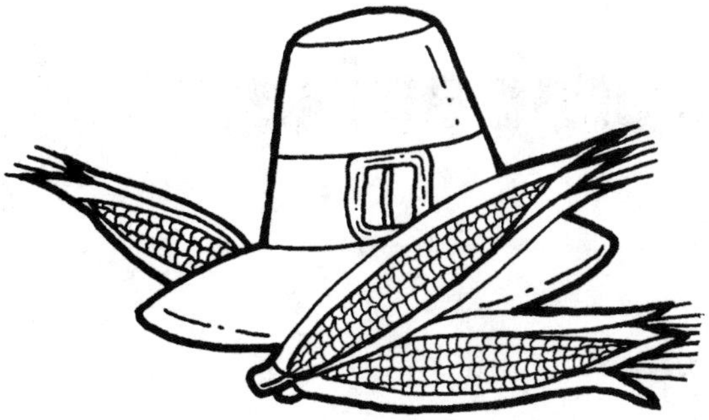

Date_____

Dear Families,

_____

_____

_____

_____

_____

_____

_____

_____

_____

_____

_____

_____

_____

_____

_____

_____

_____

_____

_____

_____

_____

_____

_____

December News

Date_____

Dear Families,

_____

_____

_____

_____

_____

_____

_____

_____

_____

_____

_____

_____

_____

_____

_____

_____

_____

_____

_____

_____

_____

_____

_____

_____

_____

_____

January News

Date_____

Dear Families,

_____
_____
_____
_____
_____
_____
_____
_____
_____
_____
_____
_____
_____
_____
_____
_____
_____
_____
_____
_____

_____

_____

February News

Date_____

Dear Families,

_____

_____

_____

_____

_____

_____

_____

_____

_____

_____

_____

_____

_____

_____

_____

_____

_____

_____

_____

_____

_____

_____

_____

_____

                      _____

                      _____

March News

Date_____

Dear Families,

_____

_____

_____

_____

_____

_____

_____

_____

_____

_____

_____

_____

_____

_____

_____

_____

_____

_____

_____

_____

_____

April News

Date_____

Dear Families,

_____

_____

_____

_____

_____

_____

_____

_____

_____

_____

_____

_____

_____

_____

_____

_____

_____

_____

_____

_____

                            _____

                            _____

May News

Date_____

Dear Families,

_____

_____

_____

_____

_____

_____

_____

_____

_____

_____

_____

_____

_____

_____

_____

_____

_____

_____

_____

_____

_____

_____

_____

June News

Date_____

Dear Families,

_____

_____

_____

_____

_____

_____

_____

_____

_____

_____

_____

_____

_____

_____

_____

_____

_____

_____

_____

_____

_____

July News

Date_____

Dear Families,

_____

_____

_____

_____

_____

_____

_____

_____

_____

_____

_____

_____

_____

_____

_____

_____

_____

_____

_____

_____

_____

_____

August News

Date_____

Dear Families,

_____

_____

_____

_____

_____

_____

_____

_____

_____

_____

_____

_____

_____

_____

_____

_____

_____

_____

                              _____

                              _____

The world belongs to the energetic.

—*Ralph Waldo Emerson*

Play

When a Child Plays

Outside play is an extension of the classroom and should be carefully thought out for the children's learning experience. Outside play is not to give the teachers a break. It is healthy for the children to go outside whenever possible. Outside play should occur at least one time a day, even on days that are not always ideal. Spending a little time in the rain, snow, and/or wind is good for children—just be sure they are dressed appropriately.

Riding Toys

When children play on riding toys, they learn strength, balance, and large muscle coordination. Children use their energy in a constructive manner. They develop concepts of speed, direction, and location. Children use their imaginations as they pretend to be different characters and to make different "road" noises. Language development is enhanced with this kind of play. Riding toys allow children to learn to negotiate, to take turns, and to solve problems. They gain self-confidence in learning and mastering new skills.

Climbing Equipment

When using climbing equipment, children learn how their bodies move. They develop concepts like *up/down, high/low, in/out/around, over/under,* and *backwards/sideways/forward*. Children develop a sense of safety when learning to avoid moving swings or jumping from monkey bars and landing safely in the sand. Arm and leg strength is enhanced. Problem-solving skills are developed when learning to get from one place to another. From this, a sense of exploration grows.

Ball Play

When playing with balls, children learn eye-hand coordination from throwing and catching them. Kicking balls encourages balance. The teacher can also incorporate cooperative play with another child when playing with balls. It is a natural thing to bring children together. Language concepts learned when playing with balls are *big/little, rolling/bouncing, near/far,* and *round/not round*.

Swings

When swinging, children are developing their vestibular system. This system helps us to recognize where our bodies are in relation to other people or objects. Children develop hand strength and upper body strength as well. Cause and effect concepts are applied when they learn that if they let go, they will fall off the swing. Children learn to share and to take turns. Safety issues learned when going around moving swings and giving pushes to other children are encouraged. Language concepts that are utilized in swinging are *high/low, fast/slow,* and *push*. The imagination can be used to play in the swing area if others are not swinging in the swing.

Safety

On pages 135–138 you will find information to help you provide safe, outdoor play environments.

Outside Activities

Tire Swings

There are a variety of ways to use a tire swing. Children can sit in them in a variety of ways such as straddling, lying, or standing. They can also move in different directions: side to side, back and forth, diagonally, and around. Children can swing in a steady rhythm or in a jerky manner. They can lie on the swing and pick up objects from the ground or throw objects from a moving swing into a target. Swings also encourage language when the teacher swings with a child or two children ride a swing together.

Easel Painting

Painting at easels is fun when done outside. Smocks and clean up are easy and the fence can be turned into a clothesline. Hang the art with clothespins on the fence.

Bubbles

Put bubbles in spill-proof containers or large tubs that will not spill easily. Use berry baskets as wands. Fill the sand table with bubble solution, locate large and small wands, and then blow, blow, blow!

Finger Painting

Finger-paint on trays or on easels. This is great fun outside when done on picnic tables. Cleanup is easy and fun when it can be hosed off.

Painting

Use large paintbrushes or rollers and water to "paint" the walls of the center or sidewalk. Riding toys, tables, and climbing equipment can always use a "paint" touch up.

Parachute Play

Parachute play is a great way to get everyone to play together. Place balls in the center of the area. Children love to run under the lifted parachute or make a tent and sit beneath it.

Outside Activities (cont.)

Obstacle Course

This is very enjoyable on the playground. Use indoor equipment borrowed from the classroom to mix with the outdoor equipment already outside. Set up the course so that children can crawl under, climb over, hop on, step through, throw balls into, run, walk, hop, walk sideways or backwards, crabwalk, and/or wheelbarrow walk. Imitation is the best teacher, so get up and run the course in front of the children. Extra personnel or adult volunteers can help to supervise the safety of the obstacle course.

Sensory Tables

Sensory tables can be filled with dirt and water. This combination, of course, makes a delightful mud. Have smocks available for this play. Birdseed and shaving cream are also fun to use outdoors. If desired, remove the child's shirt to keep the mess to a minimum.

Chalk

Large and small chalk available to children is a great way to practice fine motor and imagination skills. Place the bucket of chalk on a large area of sidewalk and just start "chalking." In a few minutes, little artists will surround you.

Balls

Have balls available in all sizes for throwing and kicking games. A hoop placed at child level and attached to a stable surface encourages throwing balls through a hoop.

Pools

In warm weather, fill a child-sized pool with water. Remember that an adult must be posted at this pool at all times when any amount of water is in it. It is possible for a child to drown in even an inch (2.5 cm) of water, so the greatest caution should be taken for a safe, pleasurable experience.

Playground Safety Checklist

General Considerations

All play structures for young children should be . . .

- well finished with smooth corners to eliminate splinters and cuts.
- constructed with no protruding elements such as nails or steel rods that might cause injury to children.
- placed on a shock-absorbing surface such as sand, pea gravel, or granulated pine bark. (No equipment that takes children off the ground should be on a hard surface.)

Access to Slides and Climbing Structures

All structures should . . .

- provide children with a good balance and secure handholds as they climb up and down.
- have a safe, comfortable resting space where there is a transition to another activity (e.g., the platform at the top of a slide).
- sometimes provide other climbing options besides stairs and ladders. (Stairs are enjoyed by younger children but older children like to have the opportunity to climb in other ways such as graduated platforms or rope-netting poles.)

Climbing Structures

Do not build or buy equipment for young children from which a vertical fall height of greater than eight feet (2.5 m) is possible. When structures bring children to levels 30 inches (80 cm) or more off the ground, the structures must have . . .

- protective siding corresponding to the age and size of the children. For children ages three to six years, siding should be 28–32 inches (70–80 cm) high.
- siding that is either solid or made of vertical boards to inhibit climbing on the siding.
- no horizontal bars that allow children to climb higher than the planned height.
- safe ways of getting from one part of the structure to another.
- a good hand grip with a rung diameter approximately 1.5 inches (4 cm).
- smooth and rounded corners, when made of wood.
- platforms with solid flooring so that sand and grit cannot fall onto children playing below.
- a design that does not place a slide and ladder parallel to each other. This prevents children from jumping from the ladder to the slide.
- no horizontal ladder or bar above or adjacent to a slide that could allow a child swinging on the ladder or bar to kick a child descending the slide.
- no open platforms adjacent to a swing.
- boards and enclosure bars that will not allow children to get their heads or arms stuck between them. Openings of 4.25–9 inches (11–23 cm) can cause fatal head entrapments.
- firm, safe connections in any rope-climbing nets or suspension nets that are used.
- soft surfaces directly below and about 80 inches (2 m) beyond the equipment to provide a safety zone.

Playground Safety Checklist (cont.)

Slides

All slides should have . . .

- an enclosed "takeoff" platform at the top, making it virtually impossible for a child to fall.
- a barrier across the top of the slide that encourages a child to sit down to slide.
- siding three to six inches (8–15 cm) high along the length of the sliding surface to prevent children from rolling off.
- no bars along the siding that can catch outstretched arms or legs.
- a slope of about 40 degrees that will provide speed without endangering the child.
- a run-off lip at the base that promotes a smooth landing by slowing the child to a walking speed upon exit from the slide. The lip's edge should be rounded.
- single-sheet stainless steel construction wherever possible, with longer slides carefully constructed to eliminate the chance of inter laid or welded joints cutting children.
- a smooth sliding surface that will not wear from frequent use.
- a safety zone that extends more than 80 inches (2 m) beyond the runoff lip.
- a safety zone along both sides of the slide that is at least 40 inches (1 m) from the protective siding of the slide.
- no metal bolts or other sharp construction braces visible on the sliding surface or along the siding.
- open areas that are not exposed to direct sun for long periods of the day. A slide should never be built with a southern exposure as surfaces will often be too hot for comfort.

Swings

All swings should have . . .

- ample space around them. Locate them in an area at least 40 feet by 20 feet (6 m x 6 m). A hedge or low fence surrounding the swings can prevent small children from running into the path of a swing.
- A-shaped supports framing the swing seats.
- no more than two seats attached to an individual frame to minimize bumping accidents.
- independent swinging seats hanging side by side and spaced at least 38 inches (1 m) apart to diminish sideways bumping.
- seats with at least 16 inches (41 cm) of ground clearance when in use.
- seats constructed of impact-absorbing materials or impact-absorbing surfaces on all contact areas.
- no hard or wooden seats.
- reliable fastening (shackles or fastening, not S-hooks) on suspension mechanisms that will not open under stress and can be secured against unauthorized loosening.
- plastic coverings over the chains.
- openings between the links of $5/16$ inches (8 mm) or less to prevent finger pinching.

Playground Safety Checklist (cont.)

Tire Swings

- No steel-belted radial tires should be used. The steel bands can eventually poke through and cause serious injury. If using such tires, make regular and thorough inspections.

- Tires should have small holes every five to six inches (12–15 cm) to allow water to drain, reducing the possibility of mosquitoes or spiders in warm weather and preventing ice in cold weather.

- In Southern climates, paint tire interiors white to discourage nesting poisonous spiders.

- Never place a single-point tire swing next to another kind of swing on the same support beam. In the event you use one-point pivot swings, be sure the swing cannot hit solid support beams or guard rails on structures.

Tunnels

- Only tunnels constructed in a straight line with no bends, junctions, or vertical access connections are acceptable.

- Tunnels must have entry and exit points above the surrounding ground level, and they must be laid to facilitate drainage.

- Internal diameter must be at least 40 inches (1 m) and the tunnel length no more than 10 feet (3 m).

Rocking Equipment

All rocking equipment should . . .

- allow the young child to initiate and control the rocking motion.

- ensure that limbs cannot be pinched or trapped in the spring of the equipment being used.

- provide the child with comfortable and secure handholds and seating positions.

- provide side-to-side as well as back-and-forth rocking motions for increased challenge.

Playground Safety Checklist (cont.)

Seesaws and Rotating Equipment

- Only seesaws that are spring-based or counter-balanced by springs should be used. Traditional seesaws can cause a spine-crushing blow when the seat hits the ground.

- Only rotating equipment with built-in mechanisms to control rotation speed is appropriate.

Paint and Finishes

- Paints, finishes, and lubricants used on playground equipment should be absolutely nontoxic. Wood preservatives should conform to accepted standards. Do not use wood treated with creosote, pentachlorophenol, or ACA.

Play Sand

Sand for sandboxes should be . . .

- 15 to 18 inches (38–45 cm) deep.

- packable when moist and able to hold shapes well.

- a balanced mixture of particles, ranging from very fine to course, with course particles no larger than 1/16 inch (1.5 mm).

- free of any sharp materials such as artificially crushed stone.

- washed so it is clean and free of clay, silt, oxides, iron, or other contaminates. (Before accepting sand delivery, test it by placing a sample in a white cloth to see if the sand stains or discolors it. Discoloration or stain indicates the sand has not been sufficiently washed.)

- maintained and disinfected on a regular basis.

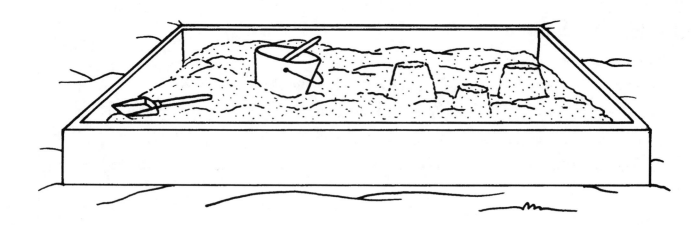

More Ideas

There are many ideas in this section of the book, and they are sure to inspire ideas of your own. Use this form to jot down your notes and other good ideas you hear from your colleagues.

My Ideas for Gross Motor Play

Play is the foundation of growth, learning, and development for children.

—Bill Page

Fine Motor Play

Many people believe that fine motor play involves only writing skills and cutting with scissors. Not so. On these pages you will find both the rationale for fine motor play and a variety of fine motor activities. (Many writing activities can be found in the art section of this book.)

We have two ways in which we learn things in life. One is through direct learning in which we discover things for ourselves; the other is indirect learning where we get information from outside ourselves (through television, computers, other people, etc.). When developing fine motor skills, we learn best directly. The term "hands-on learning" is particularly appropriate because this is how we play——with our hands on the toys.

Blocks, Cars, and Trucks

When children play with blocks, cars, and trucks, they learn concepts of *shape, size, length,* and *location*. These are important in developing reading and math skills. Children create and repeat patterns. They exercise their imaginations, express ideas, cooperate with others, solve problems, and see themselves from a different perspective—that of a giant.

Dress-up

When children play dress-up they learn to be flexible in their thinking. They learn to express themselves with words and to try out different adult roles. They solve social problems by negotiating with other children. They sort and organize playthings, make decisions, and carry out ideas with the cooperation of others. They learn to improvise and to use things in a symbolic way. They learn to use objects that represent something else. They exercise their creativity.

Puppets

When children play with puppets they learn to express themselves with words, to role-play, to use their voices with different tones, to use their imagination, and to learn how to be someone else, discovering how others may feel.

Sorting

When children do sorting activities, they learn to notice details, likenesses, and differences, and to form categories. They learn concepts of *color, size,* and *shape,* and number concepts such as *more* and *less*. They develop logical reasoning skills.

Beads

When children string beads they learn to improve their eye-hand coordination, and they learn concepts of *less, more, longer,* and *shorter*. They learn to create and reproduce patterns, and they have pride in their accomplishments.

Fine Motor Play (cont.)

Peg Boards

When children play with peg boards, they learn about one-to-one correspondence, and they make repeating patterns. They learn to develop a left-to-right progression, and they begin to learn about addition by adding one peg at a time. They learn about symmetry, shapes, order, and design. They learn about colors, and they develop eye-hand coordination.

Letter Games

When children play with letter games they learn to recognize and name upper- and lowercase letters. They learn to associate letters with sounds they represent and that letters are parts of words they say. They learn that words are what people read to them from books. They recognize their names and some other words when they are read.

Modeling Dough

When children play with clay or play dough, they learn the prereading skill of seeing shapes against a background (the table). They learn shapes, size, length, and height. Children develop small muscle strength in their fingers when squeezing, poking, rolling, and patting the dough. It not only exercises the fingers, but the imagination as well.

Helping Children with Fine Motor Trouble

Some children will have trouble with fine motor activities. Some of these children will need intervention by a therapist; however, there are activities that will help them. Here are a few:

- Use a lighted-screen toy in which the child can finish a picture by placing the colored bulbs in the screen.

- Use a clothespin to pick up cotton balls and put them into the basket. Tongs are a good alternative to the clothespin.

- Put a handful of marbles in a washtub, adding water and suds. The child then "washes" the marbles.

- Finger popping marbles across a line is great fun. Create a "marble race" with the marbles.

- Drop items into a narrow-neck bottle.

- Use finger puppets.

Fine Motor Skills

Drawing

In assessing children's fine motor skills in regard to drawing, refer to these guidelines.

- **1–2 years:** random scribbling
- **2–2.5 years:** controlled scribbling
- **2.5–3 years:** beginning to make faces
- **3.5–4 years:** adding stick arms and legs to the face
- **4 years:** adding a body to the head, arms, and legs
- **5 years:** adding houses which generally "float" on the page
- **5.5–6 years:** resting house on the paper's edge

Using Scissors

In assessing children's fine motor skills in regard to cutting, refer to the following outline. It shows the progression of cutting skills.

- **Gluing:** This is a pre-scissors skill. Successful gluing means a child can use the correct amount of glue and can cross lines to complete a project.
- **Tearing:** This involves pulling hands away from the middle to tear the paper (reciprocal), or one hand coming toward the body and the other hand pulling away (bilateral).
- **Snipping** : The width of paper is about two-thirds of the scissors' blades.
- **Fringing:** The width of paper is one inch (2.5 cm) longer than the scissors' blades.
- **Strips:** The paper is six to eight inches (15 to 22 cm) long and four to six inches (10–15 cm) wide
- **Sides:** The child cuts off one side then turns the paper to cut off another side.
- **Angles:** The child cuts and then stops in the middle of the paper, turning the paper and cutting again.
- **Rounded shapes:** The child turns and cuts the paper at the same time.
- **Curves:** The child turns the paper and cuts until he/she returns to where the cutting began.
- **Spirals:** The child cuts a spiral.

In assessing children's fine motor skills in regard to pre-writing, refer to this outline. It shows the progression of pre-writing skills.

- The child uses his/her fist to hold a crayon and makes incidental marks.
- The child imitates scribbles.
- The child makes purposeful marks.
- The child holds a writing instrument with his/her fingers (incorrectly but not fisted).
- The child draws a ball.
- The child traces a vertical line.
- The child traces a horizontal line.
- The child uses a correct grasp on a writing instrument (by age 5).

More Ideas

There are many ideas in this section of the book, and they are sure to inspire ideas of your own. Use this form to jot down your notes and other good ideas you hear from your colleagues.

My Ideas for Fine Motor Play

Children learn through all their senses to develop a sense for order and logical thoughts.

—*Maria Montessori*

Sensory Integration and Impairments

Children love the activities that are presented in the preschool setting. They sing, dance, play with sound, sights, and textures. Most children love these activities because they have effective sensory integration. They have the ability to organize the sensory information around them for use in their daily lives. When they touch something, their brains allow them to understand that, for example, "soft" is pleasant, and the child is able to respond to the soft texture in a normal, well-regulated way.

Sensory integration is the ability to take in, sort out, and connect information from the world around us. This information comes in through our senses: the sense of touch, vision, movement, hearing, smell, and taste.

Touch is the earliest sense to develop, even before birth. Touch becomes the source for emotional gratification as well as the basic building block for later perceptions.

Vision is where basic information is received through the eyes and forms the basis for visual perceptions later on.

Movement, sometimes referred to as the vestibular system, includes such things as rocking, swinging, and roughhousing experiences. It is the basis for hearing, language, and the sense of left and right. This gives children information about their bodies and how gravity affects them. This is a very powerful sense and influential in organizing the brain.

Hearing sensations are basic in building speech and language.

Smell and taste interact with the other senses to make adaptive responses.

Most children do not think about taking in the information and using it to respond to situations at home, at school, on the playground, or in social interactions. It just happens automatically. In fact, sensory integration begins in the womb and develops in an orderly sequence until it is complete by the age of 10.

Play is how a child obtains sensory input, and it is essential for motor and emotional development. Through large movements, children learn how to relate to the space around them. Through fine motor activities, children learn to use their hands and fingers effectively. Play lets a child feel competent.

If a child is unable to organize the sensory input he or she receives, then the information has little meaning. If a child becomes overexcited, sad, or hostile during play, there may be a failure in sensory motor processing, and these experiences can stop a child from learning.

Some children do not have an intact sensory ability and are unable to integrate the stimuli presented to them in everyday life. Faced with the challenge to live in the world of others whose sensorimotor systems are at a different level than theirs, these children become tense, unhappy, and confused. They refuse to participate in activities, and when they are forced to "try" something, they do so inappropriately and disrupt the flow of the classroom or lesson. At home the parents of these children are concerned because their child seems different from others, but they just cannot pinpoint what is different or why they act the way they do.

Sensory Integration and Impairments (cont.)

Children who have sensorimotor impairments are not "behavior problems"; they do not need to change their behaviors. Teachers simply need to understand how the world feels to them. An occupational therapist can help a teacher with a child who is sensorimotor impaired. The teacher can set up the classroom during free play to offer sensory play activities that help the child learn to integrate the sensory experiences of life.

Sensory integration impairment impacts learning in different ways. First, the child cannot respond to sensory information to plan and organize what he/she needs to do. Thus, the child may not learn easily. Secondly, a child's adaptive behavior may be affected. This behavior deals with the ability to respond actively and purposely to new circumstances such as new lessons that a teacher is introducing to the class. The third kind of learning that is challenged is motor learning. This is the ability to develop increasingly complex skills after one has mastered a simple one. Lastly, there is academic learning. That is the ability to acquire conceptual skills such as reading, computing, and applying what one has learned.

Some possible signs of sensory integration problems are . . .

- being overly sensitive to touch, movement, sights, and sounds
- being under-reactive to sensory stimulation
- having activity levels that are either unusually high or unusually low
- having coordination problems
- having delayed speech and language
- having delays in motor skills
- having poor organization of behavior (e.g., is impulsive and easily distracted, has poor motor planning, exhibits frustration and aggression, or withdraws when encountering failure)
- having a poor self-concept (lazy, unmotivated, stubborn, etc.).

If the teacher thinks a child may have a sensory integration disorder, an evaluation should be conducted by a qualified occupational or physical therapist. Check at a children's hospital or at a large general hospital for someone who has been trained in sensory integration, or get a listing of certified therapists by contacting:

> Sensory Integration International
> 1402 Cravens Ave.
> Torrance, California 90501
> (213) 533-8335

If a child has a sensory integration problem, he or she will not outgrow it. The longer the delay for treatment, the slower the treatment will work. The younger the brain, the more flexible and easier it is to influence.

Activities to Develop Sensory Integration

These activities are presented to guide the teacher in helping those children who have sensory challenges. However, these activities can and should be used with all preschool children. Children learn naturally through their senses, so it makes sense to use these activities daily in the classroom.

Tactile Integration

(This deals with the sense of touch.)

Water Play: Fill the kitchen sink or a plastic tub with sudsy water and include a variety of unbreakable pitchers and bottles, turkey basters, sponges, eggbeaters, and water toys. Pouring and measuring help to develop the tactile system.

Water Painting: Outdoors, provide children with buckets of water and large paintbrushes to paint walls, sidewalks, and/or fences.

Fingerpainting: Provide finger paint (it is very thick) and large areas of paper on which to indulge in this tactually-stimulating activity. If the child shuns it, encourage him or her to use one finger only.

Shaving Cream: Place a glob of shaving cream on the table and encourage the children to spread, write in, and poke the shaving cream. Show them how to "squeeze" it between their fingers. Peanut butter also works well and, unlike the shaving cream, is edible.

Feelie Box: Hide small objects in a "feelie box" (a box that has holes in the sides to put your hands through; the top of the box is sealed). See if the child can find the objects and then tell you what they are.

Oral Activities: These are activities that include tasting and licking. Stickers are an enjoyable way to encourage children to lick.

Cooking Activities: These activities include those that require stirring, hand mixing, and tasting. Yum!

Vestibular Integration

(This is the sensory system that responds to changes in head position and body movements through space. The receptors are in the inner ear.)

Rolling: Cut out the bottom of a large cardboard box so that each end is open. Let the child crawl into the box and roll down a hill, incline, or the hallway. You can also roll up in a piece of carpet, bubble wrap, a sheet or blanket. Be sure that the child's head is not enclosed in a blanket, sheet, carpet, or bubble wrap. Keep in mind that the child's airways must be unrestricted at all times.

Swinging: Encourage the child to swing. (Please do not force swinging.) Gentle linear movement helps to build vestibular systems. If height is a problem, provide a low, flat surface that can swing in all directions.

Activities to Develop Sensory Integration (cont.)

Vestibular Integration *(cont.)*

Sliding: A child can slide on a slide in many directions: facedown, faceup, backwards, and more.

Jumping: Mini-trampolines are enjoyable to have in the classroom. Jumping is hard work but invigorating!

Rocking: This can be done on a rocking horse or in a chair.

Ball Sitting: Sitting on a firm ball helps to develop balance.

Walking Up and Downstairs: If there are stairs available, instruct the child to walk up the steps to enter a section of the room and downstairs to leave.

Proprioceptive Integration

(This is the perception of internal bodily conditions, such as muscle contraction.)

Carrying: Heavy loads help the body to know where weight is placed. Messages are then sent to the brain.

Pushing and Pulling: These activities use the muscles and joints for hard work.

Hanging by the Arms: This is done safely on the playground where an adult can stand near the child to prevent any injury from falling.

Jump and Dive: Pile several large cushions in a row on a carpeted area. Invite the children to jump and dive into the soft cushions.

Turtle Walk: Place a beanbag on the child's back (like a turtle shell on a turtle) while on all fours. Walk like a turtle.

Body Hugs: Have the children sit on the floor very close to each other, and tell them to reach as far as they can around the person in front. They should then hug and squeeze.

Paper Tearing: Give the children pieces of paper which they can tear into little pieces. Coordinate an art project with this activity so the children can use what they have torn.

Sensorimotor Skills

(These develop the ability to take in messages and to act upon them.)

Flour Sifting: Spread newspaper on the floor and scoop cups of flour into a sifter. Help the child to turn the sifter handle.

Small Things: Color with small bits of crayons, play with small blocks, and make small jigsaw puzzles. Be sure to note the age appropriateness of the toy and child.

Cutting: Provide many opportunities to use scissors. Snip as a start before cutting on solid lines. Just give children scissors and paper, and they are off!

Stringing and Lacing: Provide shoelaces and yarn with the ends taped. Use these for stringing objects to make bracelets and necklaces or to hang items from the ceiling. Coordinate your theme with lacing projects. For example, if football is the theme, cut out and punch holes in football shapes. Color and lace the footballs. Hang these in the room.

Activities to Develop Sensory Integration (cont.)

Motor Planning

(This is how movements are planned.)

Obstacle Courses: Set up a room in the center where items can be arranged and rearranged to provide a variety of obstacles. Use stairs, balance beams, and other equipment. Crawl through tunnels to challenge the body into different positions. Try this in bare or stocking feet.

Rock and Roll Body Parts: Play music to see what different parts of the body the children can use to tap out the beat.

Animal Walk: Pretend to be animals and see how they walk through their habitats.

Marble Painting: Line a tray or tin with a few dabs of finger paint. Put marbles on the tray, and with the child using both hands (one on each side of the tray), roll the marbles around the tray. This makes very pretty wrapping paper.

Auditory Activities

(These deal with the sense of hearing.)

Listen: Become an active listener.

Speed: Slow down your speech. Shorten your sentences and requests when speaking to the children.

Time: Let the child have extra time to answer your questions.

Nonverbal Gestures: Reward the child using nonverbal gestures such as smiles and praise.

Attention: Talk to the children while they are engaged in activities, not at them.

Rhythm Sticks: Use rhythm sticks to help with auditory memory. Tap out beats and have the children repeat the sequence and patterns.

Fill-in-the-Blank: Tell part of a story line and stop. Encourage everyone to take a turn to finish the story.

Visual Activities

(These deal with the sense of sight.)

Flashlight Fun: Use a flashlight in a darkened (not completely dark) room and find different things with the light. The child or teacher can find the items and the others can label them.

Shape Up: Draw shapes in pudding, shaving cream, fingerpaints, etc. This can be done with dough or clay as well.

Pegboard Designs: Purchase cards with designs, or create your own that the children can copy.

Puzzles, Puzzles, and More Puzzles: Puzzles are always excellent tools for developing a variety of skills, including visual sensory integration.

Sensorimotor Unit Ideas

The emphasis of these ideas is not to master the activities but to have each child be involved actively in the sensory stimulation.

The following is a list of materials to collect for use throughout the unit activities.

- masking tape
- big red balls
- ring toss
- old terry towel torn into small washrags

- fleece or foam balls
- clothesline or rope
- flashlight

- sheet or cotton blanket
- bean bags
- chalk

Rolling

- Lying on their backs, with arms on the floor over their heads, instruct the children to rock from side to side for 30 to 60 seconds.
- Children can lie on the carpet and rub their bodies and extremities on it.
- Let the children roll across the room any way they know how.
- Have the children roll across the room with arms over their heads.
- Have the children roll across room with arms down at their sides.
- With arms over their heads, instruct the children to hold onto a ball and roll across the room.
- Make a chalk mark on a carpet square and have them rub it off with their hands, forearms, feet, etc.
- Lying on their backs, have them curl up like a ball and hold for a count of ten. Gradually increase the number.
- Have children roll over an object (another student, incline, etc.).
- Have children roll under an object (table, a sheet suspended over chairs, etc.).
- Children roll between objects.
- Children rub arms and other body parts with washcloths.
- Children roll onto stomach, side, back, and reverse procedure.
- Have children roll to commands such as stop and go.
- Have children roll with a beanbag in hand, arms over head, and then throw the beanbag at a target suspended two feet above the ground (wastebasket, dart board, target, etc.).
- Children lie on the ground on their backs and pretend to be angels. They then roll on their stomachs and repeat.
- Have children roll with a beanbag between their knees.
- Children roll "in" an object (boxes with ends cut out, tunnel, etc.).
- Children lie on their stomachs and hold onto their ankles, rocking forward and backward.
- Children lie on their backs and look up at the ceiling. With lights out, shine a light across the ceiling. Instruct the children to point to and follow the light with one arm and then the other. Then they can use one leg at a time. Make patterns with light: horizontal, vertical, and circular.

Sensorimotor Unit Ideas (cont.)

Rolling *(cont.)*

- Put powder on arms, legs, feet, etc., and have the children rub it off with washcloths.

- Tie a rope firmly across the room (or held tightly by two adults). Have the children lie on their backs and one at a time pull themselves across the room.

- If the children will tolerate this, have them roll across the room with a paper bag over their heads.

- Instruct them to lie on their stomachs and have them toss balls into a basket. The ball should be large enough so that they must hold on with both hands.

- Ask the children to lie on their backs and toss the large balls at a target. They should raise their heads to see the target and aim.

- Do a duck walk. (Squat with hands behind seat to look like a tail and waddle across the room.)

- Do a crocodile walk. (Belly crawl with a growling sound.)

- Do a crab walk. (Walk on all fours, upside down. Go forwards, backwards, and sideways.)

- Do a bear walk. (Lean over at the waist and with hands on the floor, walk across the room, stomping the hand and foot of the same side at the same time.)

- Do a chicken walk. (Place hands under armpits to look like wings and squatting down, walk across the room, cackling.)

Crawling

- Instruct the children to lie on their stomachs and crawl across the room like crocodiles.

- Have them lie on their stomachs with their hands under their chin. Instruct them to lift one leg at a time as high as possible without rolling over on their sides. Have them lift their legs separately, then together.

- Ask them to lie on their stomachs and creep like turtles, very slowly.

- Have them lie on their stomachs and creep like crocodiles going after something to eat very quickly.

- They can lie on their stomachs and crawl across room, pivot on their stomachs, and return.

- Instruct them to crawl on their stomachs across the room backwards (feet first).

- Have them spin around on their bellies in a circle.

- Ask them to crawl up to a tape line on the floor and roll the rest of the way across the room.

- Be angels in the snow and have them move "this arm," "this leg," etc., by pointing to, but not touching, the body part.

Sensorimotor Unit Ideas (cont.)

Crawling *(cont.)*

- Have the children crawl on a trail (zigzag, circle, square, etc.).
- The children can scoot on their backs forward and backward.
- The children make a tunnel by bending at the waist and touching their hands on the floor. Another child crawls through the tunnel without touching the child.
- Have the children wheelbarrow race.
- Use scooter boards:
  —Ask them to spin around on their stomachs in both directions.
  —Instruct them to scoot across the room on their stomachs.
  —On their stomachs, they can follow a trail on the floor made with tape.
  —With feet against the wall, have them push off and glide as far as possible.
  —On their backs, the children can put their feet against the wall and push off.

Creeping

- In a hands and knees position, the children spin around as quickly as possible in both directions.
- Have the children lie on their stomachs and push up with their arms. Allow them to keep their knees on the ground.
- With the children lying on their backs, the teacher names a body part and the children gently move that part only. (e.g., right little finger, chin, foot, etc.).
- While the children are standing, the teacher calls a body part for them to find. For example, they put their elbows together, feet apart, touch one elbow, put knees together, touch right knee to left hand, etc.
- Have them creep with a washrag between their shoulder and chin, forwards, backwards, and sideways.
- The children can creep while pushing a ball along across the room with only their heads.
- On hands and knees, lined up side by side (sets of two) with a tape line between them and by keeping all fours on the floor, have them try to push the other one off balance without crossing the line.
- Have them, while on hands and knees, rotate their heads from side to side, looking at the ceiling and then at their knees, keeping arms and legs firm.
- Extend a rope across the room. Start up high and gradually lower. Have the children crawl under the rope without touching it (eventually to do a belly crawl).
- Use scooters:
  —Kneeling on the scooter spin around in circles and then reverse.
  —Kneeling on the scooter, move forwards, backwards, and then sideways.
  —Kneel and follow various trails.

Sensorimotor Unit Ideas (cont.)

Creeping *(cont.)*

- In pairs, have the children lie on their backs with knees bent and their feet touching. See who can push the other over.
- On hands and knees, ask them to lift one hand and balance for a count of ten. Repeat with the other hand and shake the hand all about.
- Do as above, but use legs.
- Have the children do wheelbarrows following a tape trail on the floor.

Sitting

- In a tailor-sitting (cross legged) position, have them rotate their bodies from the waist in a circular motion, first with hands flat on the floor and then without hands (arms folded or over the head).
- In a tailor-sitting position, instruct the children to slump over forwards and then return to a straight sitting posture.
- In a long-sitting position (legs straight and out in front), instruct them to slump over forwards, attempt to touch their heads to their knees, and return to straight sitting.
- In a tailor-sitting position while blindfolded, have them sway from side to side. They can then rotate their bodies in a circular motion, and then do the same with their heads only.
- Lying on their backs, have them raise their legs in the air to pump them in circles like on a bicycle.
- In a long-sitting position, instruct them to lie down and then sit up and curl into a tight ball.
- In a tailor-sitting position, have them put their hands behind their necks and sway from side to side.
- Partners stand back to back with elbows linked. From this position, they can attempt to sit down slowly and then try to stand up.
- From a long-sitting position, the children can place their hands on the floor at the sides of their hips. Pressing down, they can straighten their arms until their buttocks are off the floor and then hold there for a count of five.
- From a long-sitting position, have the children stretch to touch their right hands to their left toes and left hands to their right toes.
- Play musical chairs with chairs and stools of various heights so that the children must adjust accordingly.
- Using scooters:
    - Ask the children to tailor-sit on a scooter and to propel themselves forward with their hands. Have them go in circles in both directions.
    - While sitting like a tailor, have them hold a hula hoop while an adult pulls them.
    - Sitting like a tailor, have them scoot forward, backward, and sideways.

Sensorimotor Unit Ideas (cont.)

Kneeling

- Suspend a ball from the ceiling. Have two children kneel opposite one another and have them bat the ball with one hand, taking turns doing this.
- While kneeling, the children can fold their arms and rock from side to side.
- While kneeling, the children can fall forward onto their hands and return.
- With partners in kneeling positions, instruct the children to face each other and hold hands. They rock forward, backward, and side to side.
- From a kneeling position, have student partners "stand" shoulder to shoulder and try to push each other off balance, using only their shoulders.
- On their knees, instruct the children to walk forward, backward, and sideways.
- While kneeling, have them kick their feet up and down. With feet spread apart and then together, have them keep their knees together.
- Kneeling, the children can place their right legs foot down in front of their bodies and count to five. Repeat with the left leg.
- Children kneel and sit on their heels, hands on the floor. They then lean forward, sliding their hands out in front of them until their chest touches their knees. In this position, they can swing their arms to the left and then to the right.
- Instruct the children to face the wall in a kneeling position. With their hands on the wall, they can "walk" sideways in both directions.
- Kneeling, the children can hold both hands over their heads and sway from side to side.

Standing

- Standing independently, have the children swing one leg forward, backward, in and out, in a circular motion, and repeat on the other leg.
- Keeping their backs against the wall, have them slide back up and down and (wide apart) rock forward and backward.
- Instruct the children to walk backwards in and out of an obstacle course.
- While they are standing on a spot on the floor with their eyes closed, ask the children to point to the ceiling, floor, teacher, etc.
- Have the children lean against the wall and roll across the wall.
- Have the children face the wall, touching the wall with their nose, ear, forehead, etc.
- With their backs to the wall, have the children walk sideways along the wall.
- While the children are standing on the floor, have them rock on their feet, going from toes to heels, and repeating several times.
- Have the children walk "small" then walk "tall" (squatting to tiptoes).
- With their sides against the wall, have the children walk around the room.
- Put a tape or chalk line on the floor and have the children walk forward on the line, backwards, do crossover steps over the line, and walk sideways on the line.

More Ideas

There are many ideas in this section of the book, and they are sure to inspire ideas of your own. Use this form to jot down your notes and other good ideas you hear from your colleagues.

My Ideas for Sensory Integration Play

What we have to learn to do, we learn by doing.

—*Aristotle*

All About Play

Play is how children learn! Children discover things themselves through trial and error. As adults we need to encourage their play, not direct it. Children do most things out of curiosity. They become actively engaged in play for the pure enjoyment of it. Practically everything a child does is play. It can be joyful, serious, solitary, or social. Play is frequent, repetitive, and always creative. Play helps children to understand what they see and experience in the real world. Preschoolers move from the make-believe symbols in play to the symbols of reading, math, and other high-level skills.

Play should be fun. While children are having fun, play is how they acquire, practice, and master skills. They strengthen their small and large muscles and form attitudes toward others and about themselves.

Play should always be a positive time. When children play, they should feel that they are successful. Success promotes a child's self-confidence and increases the desire to do and learn more.

Most children go through a sequence of developmental skills as they learn to play, and play is the primary way to develop these motor skills. Here is a sequence of developmental play skills.

Developmental Play Skills

I. Random and Exploratory Play

This play occurs when a child shakes, mouths, bangs, and turns over toys and other objects. A child explores objects by tasting, looking at, listening to, moving, and feeling them with his or her whole body. (To encourage random and exploratory play, give the child opportunities to explore the objects/toys, using their different senses. The toys must be safe, nontoxic, colorful, and interesting.)

Hearing: Talk about objects as you play with them. Talk about the sounds they make, pointing out how different objects make different sounds.

Sight: Be sure that the child is looking at the objects and turning them around to see them from all angles. It may be necessary to touch the child gently on the face to turn his/her attention to the object.

Touch: Help the child to feel each object all over. Let the child hold the toy. Rub the object against the child's cheek. Be sure that there are opportunities to feel the different textures and temperatures.

Movement: Have the children shake each object, swing it, and hit it on the table or the floor. Let the child throw soft spongy objects when appropriate and run after them to retrieve them. Let the child push, pull, and move objects. Give the child spoons, pots, and pans to bang.

Taste and Smell: Provide the child with foods or other things that have a smell. Instruct the child to place the items near his or her nose. If it is food, let the child lick or taste it. (Be sure that other things children explore with their mouths are not dirty or dangerous.)

All About Play (cont.)

II. Early Functional Play

This play occurs when a child begins to use objects the way they were meant to be used. For example, the child will use a brush to brush hair, but he or she will also use the same brush for other things. The child will roll a ball, stack blocks, listen to a toy phone, and use a washcloth to wash things.

To encourage early functional play, be sure to stop a minute to watch the child play appropriately and give the child some attention and a smile. It is very important to reward the child's spontaneous play with attention and praise. When a child is introduced to a new toy, take the object and use it appropriately and use words to describe what you are doing with it. For example, use the comb to comb hair and say, "Comb hair," "I am combing hair," or, "I comb hair. Here, you comb hair," and give the child the comb to use. If the child does not use it appropriately, you can gently put your hand over the child's hand and help him or her to comb the hair appropriately.

III. Later Functional Play

This type of play occurs when a child uses most toys and objects appropriately. The child will be able to respond to the request, "Show me what goes on your foot," by picking up the shoe or pointing to a picture of a shoe.

To encourage later functional play, begin to structure play. Play a "listening game" wherein they try to guess what object made the sound they heard. Have a "mystery box" where a toy is put in the box and the child is asked to name the toy.

IV. Creative-Symbolic Play

Creative-symbolic play happens when a child begins to use symbols in play such as pretending that a box is a train or a hairbrush is a telephone.

To encourage creative-symbolic play, give the child opportunities to play with other children slightly above the child's play level. Provide the child with dolls, blocks, dishes, puppets, dress-up clothes, and paper and crayons to play with alone or with an adult.

V. Imaginative Play

Imaginative play happens when the child uses increased creativity and imagination in play. The child may play with imaginary friends or pretend to be someone else. The child will act out familiar household routines when playing "house."

To encourage imaginative play development, it is appropriate to provide objects and toys appropriate to the child's skills. The teacher or parent can read stories to the child and provide the child with items to be used to act out real-life situations such as doctor kits, dress-up clothes, and puppets.

All About Play (cont.)

Play and Fine Motor Development

Several art and play activities involve fine motor skills. Snack time does as well. Here are some materials that you may want to have in the classroom to encourage fine motor development.

Infants: busy box, mirrors, mobiles, nesting containers, visual rattles, and brightly-colored, dangling objects

Toddlers: blocks, crayons and paper, cutting and pasting shapes, nesting containers, hammer toys, pegs and pegboards, shape sorters, simple puzzles, and books

Preschoolers: beads, books, lacing cards, lotto cards, matching cards, paper, pencils, crayons, pegs and boards, puzzles, threading toys, simple games, and board games

Other useful toys you might want to add include puppets, sand/mud/water activities, all kinds of paints, clay, play dough, chalk, Tinker Toys, bristle blocks, bubbles, doll houses, workbenches, musical instruments, easels, scissors, housekeeping toys, and cause/effect toys.

Tips for Playing with Children

When playing with children, here are some things to remember.

- Talk to the children in a warm and friendly voice.
- Talk to the children in short phrases and sentences.
- Talk to the children clearly.
- Wait a few seconds after you speak so that the children have a chance to talk back to you.
- Use what a child likes to do and they will respond to the play. Then you can expand on what they like.
- Repeat often what they play. Young children need a great deal of repetition to master an activity.
- Do not expect the children to learn right away. Activities should be varied and then repeated often.
- Show the children you are interested in them and give them your attention.
- Enjoy yourself.
- Give lots of hugs, pats, and smiles.
- Have fun with the children.

Now, go play!

Play Skill Guidelines

It is beneficial to teachers to learn how to observe what kinds of play skills each child utilizes. The skills listed here are only guidelines since not all children go through the same steps or sequence.

1. Pretending with objects
   a. does not use objects to pretend
   b. uses real objects
   c. substitutes objects for other objects
   d. uses imaginary objects

2. Role-playing
   a. does not role-play
   b. says what is being pretended
   c. imitates actions of role

3. Verbalizing play scenario
   a. does not verbalize during play
   b. uses words to describe imaginary objects and actions
   c. uses words to create an imaginary play scenario

4. Verbal communications during play
   a. talks only to self during play
   b. talks only to adults in play
   c. talks with peers in play

5. Persistence in play
   a. plays for less than five minutes
   b. plays for six to nine minutes
   c. plays for 10 minutes or longer

6. Interactions
   a. plays alone
   b. plays only with adults
   c. plays with one child, always the same child
   d. plays with one child, but can be different children
   e. plays with two or three children together

7. Entrance to a play group
   a. does not attempt to enter play group
   b. forces self into the play group
   c. stands near the group and watches
   d. imitates behavior of the group
   e. gets the attention of another child before commenting

8. Conflict management
   a. gives in easily
   b. uses force to solve conflicts
   c. seeks adult assistance
   d. imitates verbal solutions heard from adults
   e. uses words when reminded
   f. initiates use of words
   g. accepts reasonable compromises

9. Turn-taking
   a. refuses to take turns
   b. leaves toys unattended and protests when others pick them up
   c. gives up toy easily if finished with it
   d. gives up toy easily if another child asks for it
   e. takes turns if directed by an adult
   f. asks for turn but does not wait for response
   g. suggests taking turns and will take and give turns

10. Support of peers
   a. shows no interest in peers
   b. directs attention to distress of peers
   c. offers help
   d. encourages or praises peers

Characteristics of Good Toys

Choosing Toys

When choosing classroom toys, keep these guidelines in mind.

All toys should . . .

- be as free of detail as possible.
- be versatile in use.
- be easily comprehended.
- have large, easily manipulated parts.
- encourage cooperative play.
- involve child in play, including large muscles.
- have material that is warm and pleasant to touch.
- be durable.
- work as intended.
- be safe.
- be generous in proportions and quantity.
- help the child learn how to reason.

Recommended Toys

The following toys are highly recommended for the preschool setting. Before each toy is a descriptor that speaks to the skill enhanced by the toy.

- building coordination: *sewing cards, blocks*
- developing creativity: *blocks, art materials, sand*
- self-correcting: *puzzles, stacking toys*
- developing perception skills: *lotto, dominoes*
- building large and small motor skills: *balls, push toys, pull toys, toys to climb on*
- encouraging reasoning, problem-solving, and creative thinking: *puzzles*
- encouraging language development: *puppets, dress-up, clothes, cars*
- nurturing self-discovery: *art materials, magnifying glasses, water, sand*

Children enjoy playing with all types of toys. A girl likes to play with cars and trucks, just as a boy enjoys playing with dolls. Remember, however, that all children need people interactions to make the toys the most effective. How teachers play with children makes all the difference in how and what they are learning. Be sure that the play—regardless of the toy—is fun and child directed.

Different Types of Play

Block Play

Soft blocks are usually the first sets of blocks children use. They pile them up and knock them down, and they will not hurt the children. For preschoolers, they usually are not interested in the color of the blocks but rather in their shapes and sizes. The blocks should fit together so that if two small triangle blocks were connected they would be the same size as the square block. Blocks teach volume, size, and multiplication skills.

At the age of two, children usually stack the blocks and then knock them down again and again. At the age of four, they make more definite structures with the blocks.

Stages of Block Play

1. carries block around
2. makes rows of blocks
3. makes simple bridges
4. encloses a space or object
5. makes decorative block patterns
6. names the block structures in dramatic play
7. copies structures they know or have seen

Dramatic Play

Dramatic play is very important to young children because it nurtures a variety of skills while bringing them tremendous pleasure and countless hours of imagination. It is important to change the dramatic-play area when the children appear bored with the materials. Children will not play appropriately in the area when they are not stimulated. By adding new props to the area, new interest is developed.

Over time, a teacher can gather props to make theme boxes for the dramatic-play area. Theme box ideas include the following:

- **Office workers:** pads of paper, typewriter, pencil holders, pens and pencils, stamps (music and book stamps that come in the mail work well), stapler, scotch tape, envelopes, hole punchers, and pictures of office workers
- **Flower shop:** flower and garden magazines, small garden tools, garden hats, gloves, aprons, plastic flowers, vases, styrofoam squares, baskets, cash register, play money, and pictures of flowers
- **Beach party:** beach towels, sunglasses, hats, empty suntan lotion bottles, small radio, plastic fish, fish net, fishing pole, inner tubes, umbrellas, beach balls, picnic basket, picnic blanket, plastic food, shells, and pictures of the beach and ocean
- **Veterinarian office:** Small stuffed animals, small rolls of cloth bandages, adhesive tape, cotton balls, stethoscope, disposable masks, magnifying glass, pet comb and brush, thermometer, pictures of animals

Different Types of Play (cont.)

Dramatic Play (cont.)

- **Beauty shop:** smocks, snap-in curlers, hand-held hairdryers with cords cut off, towels, curling irons with cords cut off, bobby pins, hair clips, empty spray bottles, empty shampoo bottles, mirrors, ribbons, bows, telephone, and pictures of hairstyles

- **Sporting goods store:** backpacks, boots, heavy socks, helmets, baseball caps, gloves, shoes, various types of balls, headbands, tennis rackets, goggles, ski caps, scuba diving fins, snorkels, hand-held weights, and pictures of sports

- **Camping:** plastic bugs, wood for fire, water bottles, pillows, fly swatter, small tent, frying pan, spatula, sunglasses, small cooler, flashlight, grill, paper plates, utensils, sleeping bags, binoculars, fishing poles, coffee pot, plastic food, and pictures of camping outdoors

Other theme box ideas are a bakery, gas station, repair shop, hardware store, grocery store, fast-food restaurant, doctor/nurse, police station, fire station, post office, dentist office, pizza parlor, and an ice cream store. The children will show what interests them.

Theme boxes can also be used for outside play as well. Put together outdoor boxes such as these:

- PVC pipes and elbows to be used in sand and water areas

- plastic hula hoops to jump in, roll around, crawl through, and more

- painting items like buckets, aprons, several brushes in various sizes, water, paint, chalk, dish soap, and paper

- various squirt bottles

- buckets, shovels, pots, and pans

- cars, trains, and trucks

- outdoor gardening supplies, including watering cans, small hoses, small rakes, child size gardening tools, gloves, kneeling pads, and hats

- large and small blocks and plastic animals, people, and cars

Use your imagination and develop your own "Theme Boxes" to use inside and outside. Simply begin to save everything! You never know when it will come in handy.

Sand and Water Play

For sand play, purchase "play" sand found at most hardware/home-supply stores all year round. This sand is clean, white, and sanitized for children to use.

Water in the water table must be changed daily. It is a good idea to have a mat with rubber backing or some indoor-outdoor carpeting under the water table and around where the children will be standing to prevent the floor from getting slippery. Also have bath towels available for spills.

Different Types of Play (cont.)

Sand and Water Play *(cont.)*

Toys to use for sand play include the following:

- balance scale
- balloons (to fill with sand)
- beans (to mix with sand)
- berry baskets
- birthday candles
- bowls
- buckets
- colanders
- cookie cutters
- craft sticks
- cups
- dinosaurs
- egg beaters
- egg cartons
- envelopes
- feathers
- flower pots
- funnels
- ice cube trays
- measuring cups and spoons
- muffin tins
- nesting toys
- nuts
- paper bags
- pasta shapes
- pie plates
- pill bottles
- plastic eggs
- plastic spoons
- plastic tubs
- rubber gloves (to fill with sand)
- salt and pepper shakers
- sand
- sand wheels
- scoops
- shells
- shovels
- small trucks
- spray bottles (to make sand wet)
- strainers
- styrofoam packing pieces
- tongs/tweezers (large ones)
- used mittens or gloves to wear
- whisks
- wooden animals, cars, blocks

Toys to use for water play include the following:

- aquarium rocks
- balloons (to fill with water)
- berry baskets
- bowls
- dosage spoons
- egg beaters
- eye droppers
- fish nets
- funnels
- measuring cups/spoons
- nesting toys
- pitchers
- plastic bottle with pin holes
- plastic eggs
- plastic fish and fishing pole
- plastic toys
- rubber gloves with pin holes (for water to leak)
- salt and pepper shakers
- scoops
- shells
- slotted spoons
- soup spoons
- sponges (in different sizes/shapes)
- squeeze bottles
- squirt bottles
- strainers
- straws
- styrofoam trays
- tongs/tweezers
- toothbrushes
- washcloths
- water wheels
- watering cans
- whisks
- wind-up toys
- wooden ladles

Items to add to the water to change the texture, appearance, or smell:

- baking soda
- beans
- birdseed
- bubble solution
- cooked spaghetti
- cornmeal
- cornstarch
- crushed ice
- dry leaves
- extracts (for smell)
- flour
- food coloring
- liquid detergent
- oatmeal
- O-shaped cereal
- pasta
- plain and colored ice cubes
- popped popcorn
- potting soil
- pumpkin pulp and seeds
- rice
- salt
- shaving cream
- wood shavings

Record of Developmental Play Skills

Child's name _____

Dates	Types and Stages of Play

More Ideas

There are many ideas in this section of the book, and they are sure to inspire ideas of your own. Use this form to jot down your notes and the good ideas you hear from your colleagues.

My Ideas for Play

Think of what a better world it would be if we all had cookies and milk about three o'clock every afternoon.

—Robert Fulghum

Let's Eat!

Food is probably the number one motivator in the world, and there are probably a million things a teacher might plan for snack time besides eating. This section of the book will address many of them.

Nutritional Needs

Children's nutritional needs are different from those of an adult. Their stomachs are not only shaped differently, they empty readily and are easily irritated. Children are very sensitive to food tastes and smells. They need nourishment at frequent intervals throughout the day. The chemical breakdown of food in a child has a direct effect on behavior. It is very important for the teacher to know which children have been up since the dawn hours before they arrived at school because such children may require a glass of juice and a few crackers to tide them over until the true snack time of the day.

Even babies who were good eaters begin to lose their appetites at around the age of two. Generally these toddlers will eat when they are hungry, but they may not eat much at any given time. Sweet foods should be limited because they fill up a child but provide very little nutritional value. Since they eat less, it is important that what children do eat is nutritious.

Snack time in preschool not only offers nutritional support to the child but a chance to engage in social and language play. While the child is engaged in this play, teachers should offer the opportunity for children to try new tastes, textures, and types of food. This is easily done when the snack time is planned to fit into the week's theme.

Snacks and Themes

Colors are ideal themes at snack times. (See also page 171.) Take, for example, the color yellow. Yellow snacks include bananas, squash, lemons, butter, scrambled eggs, pears, apples or applesauce, and cheese.

An excellent use for apples is to make applesauce. Bring in a few yellow apples, and a red, and a green apple. Introduce all the apples and discuss the colors, shapes, and smells of the apples. Cut up the red and green apples after peeling them and let the children nibble on the apple while the class proceeds to make the applesauce. Be sure to talk about the safety issues of the knife and washing of hands before cooking and eating. The more involved the children are, the more language skills will develop.

After each cooking lesson, send a copy of the recipe home with the child as a home activity. This may encourage parents to make the recipe at home and carry over the concepts taught in class that day.

Snacks can also be created to match the theme such as ants on a log (raisins on peanut butter spread in celery). Snack recipes can be found on pages 172 and 173.

Let's Eat! (cont.)

Oral Motor Development

In early growth and development (infant-toddler) one of the primary means of learning about one's own body and the environment is through the mouth. As a child continues oral exploration, skills are developed, refined, and strengthened. When the progression of oral motor development is hindered for whatever reason, there is an impact in these areas: intelligibility of speech, communication, eating and socialization with peers, and socially acceptable appearances (e.g., excessive drooling).

Below is an oral motor checklist. They are general observations. If the teacher thinks the child has charted several of the points, then it is time to consult a speech or occupational therapist. Such therapists can address the child's needs.

- drooling
- poor lip closure
- inability to suck through a straw
- difficulty blowing bubbles
- difficulty chewing solid foods
- excessive spillage of food from mouth while chewing
- poor intelligibility of speech
- obvious abnormal posture of mouth or tongue
- strong aversion to texture, consistency, or temperature of food
- aversion to toothbrushing

Classroom Activities Enhancing Oral Motor Development

1. Snack Time Activities
- Introduce various textures, temperatures, and consistencies.
- Drink malts or shakes through straws.
- Use mouth only to hold pretzels between lips or to move pretzels in mouth.
- Use tongue to pick up "O" cereal from a plate.

2. General Activities
- Blowing bubbles, whistles, kazoos, party favors, or cotton balls.
- Using straws, blow bubbles in the water or blow through a straw to propel cotton balls or balloons across the table or floor
- Hold a lip tug-o-war. A child holds the end of a licorice stick or fruit roll between his or her lips and pulls on the opposite end with his or her hands.
- Practice toothbrushing.
- Use movement/music records that incorporate oral motor demands such as yelling, screaming, and whispering.
- In front of a mirror, make faces, imitate faces, and imitate tongue movements.

Teaching Colors with Snacks

Here are a variety of snacks that can be served while learning about the various colors.

Blue
- blueberries
- gelatin
- blue gummy snacks
- food coloring in mashed potatoes or whipped cream

Red
- radishes
- strawberries
- watermelon
- cranberry sauce
- ketchup
- apples
- cherries
- tomatoes
- jam
- tomato soup
- gelatin
- red grapes
- beets
- tomato sauce
- food coloring in whipped cream or mashed potatoes

Yellow
- bananas
- lemons
- buttered toast
- applesauce
- crackers
- unpopped kernels of corn
- squash
- butter
- pineapple
- lemonade
- jam
- food coloring in whipped cream or mashed potatoes
- grapefruit
- eggs
- pears
- cheese
- lemon ice

Green
- kiwi fruit
- pears
- grapes
- gelatin
- apples
- food coloring in whipped cream or mashed potatoes

Orange
- oranges
- cantaloupe
- apricots
- food color in whipped cream or mashed potatoes
- orange juice
- pumpkin
- cheese
- carrots
- peaches
- acorn squash

Purple
- grapes
- gelatin
- plums
- grape juice
- grape jelly
- food coloring in whipped cream or mashed potatoes

Brown
- raisins
- prunes
- graham crackers
- banana bread
- apple juice
- some cereals
- toast
- gingerbread men
- shelled sunflower seeds
- chocolate milk
- mushrooms
- cinnamon and other dark spices
- apple butter
- whole wheat bread
- carob chips
- peanut butter
- food coloring in whipped cream or mashed potatoes

Try to use natural foods. These foods are versatile and can be used over and over again. Rotate the texture and kind of snack and the children will never tire of them. Most of all, talk, talk, talk about all aspects of the food. This is as important as the nutrition itself.

Snack Time Recipes

Here are some recipes that involve children in the snack time experience. You can easily use these recipes to coincide with your weekly theme. Remember to have the children wash their hands before preparing any foods.

Frozen Bananas

Ingredients:

- bananas (half banana per child)
- popsicle sticks
- small jar of honey
- small bowl of toasted wheat germ
- crushed nuts
- peanut butter
- dry milk

Directions: Cut bananas in half. Put a popsicle stick in the cut end for a handle. Do this ahead of class time and place the bananas in the freezer. When they are frozen, roll the bananas in honey, toasted wheat germ, and crushed nuts. Other toppings include peanut butter, dry milk, and honey to taste. Smear on frozen bananas. (**Note:** Children can put on gloves and do this activity with little help.)

Dip for Raw Vegetables

Ingredients:

- 1 cup (240 mL) cottage cheese
- $1/2$ cup (120 mL) sour cream
- 1 cup (240 mL) mayonnaise
- $1/2$ tsp. (2.5 mL) Worcestershire sauce
- salt and pepper to taste
- carrot sticks
- celery sticks
- raw broccoli (cut)
- raw cherry tomatoes (cut)

Directions: Place cottage cheese in a mixing bowl. Add sour cream. Beat with wire whisk so that all the children get a turn stirring. Add remaining ingredients (except the vegetables) and stir.

Peanut Butter Play Dough

Ingredients:

- 1 bottle of Karo corn syrup or 2 cups (480 mL) of honey
- 1 18 oz. (500 g) jar of peanut butter
- 1 small box of instant dry milk
- 1 box of confectioners sugar
- wax paper

Directions: Mix the ingredients together and give each child a piece of wax paper for a placemat. Let them roll the dough and eat it.

Snack Time Recipes (cont.)

Cream Cheese and Pineapple

Ingredients:

- 2 eight oz. (225 kg) packages of softened cream cheese
- 1 small can drained, unsweetened, crushed pineapple
- $\frac{1}{8}$ cup (30 mL) or less of milk
- spoons
- crackers

Directions: Mix ingredients. Add milk to make an easy-spreading consistency. Give each child a spoon and a cracker. Let the children practice their spooning skills by allowing them to scoop the cottage cheese mix onto their own crackers.

Hot vs. Cold

Ingredients:

- cocoa mix
- hot water
- ice cream

Directions: Put dry cocoa in a cup for each child. The children can taste the powder in their cups by dipping a finger. Question: Is it hot? It is cold? What does it feel like? What does it taste like? With care, pour water to make the cocoa. Stir. Give each child a scoop of ice cream and repeat the above questions.

Jack-o-Lantern Pizzas

Ingredients:

- English muffins cut in half
- sliced mozzarella cheese cut in triangles
- 1 small jar of pizza sauce

Directions: Give each child a half muffin. Children spread on the pizza sauce and add cheese for two eyes, a nose, and a mouth. Bake at 350 degrees Fahrenheit (180 degrees Celsius) until the cheese is melted.

Bird Seed

Ingredients:

- 1 cup (240 mL) each of "O" cereal, corn-rice cereal, fruit "O" cereal, and pretzel sticks
- 1 cup (240 mL) raisins
- 1 cup (240 mL) yogurt-covered raisins
- 1 cup (240 mL) chocolate chips
- 1 cup (240 mL) mini candy-coated chocolate pieces
- box of small snack baggies

Directions: This is a great activity to practice pouring and scooping. Each child can take turns pouring one cup (240 mL) of ingredients into a very large bowl. Stir. Give children a baggie and let them practice scooping the mixture with a large spoon into the baggie. Eat and enjoy.

Recipe Letter to Send Home

Dear Families,

Today we cooked as part of our snack time. Here is the recipe we made. We encourage you to make this recipe at home with your child. It is part of the theme that we have been working on this week. Enjoy!

Recipe:_____

Ingredients:

Directions:

More Ideas

There are many ideas in this section of the book, and they are sure to inspire ideas of your own. Use this form to jot down your notes and the good ideas you hear from your colleagues.

My Ideas and Recipes for Snack Time

Teachers can change lives with just the right mix of chalk and challenges.

—*Joyce A. Myers*

All About Art

Art is an important part of a child's development. Art nurtures a child's imagination and sparks individual creativity. It builds the levels of exploration and experimentation that a child allows for him or herself. It fosters in the child increased observation skills, tactile stimulation, and eye-hand coordination. Art helps the child to master visual tracking.

Art activities can be related to a theme such as colors, shapes, hard and soft, big and little, and so forth, or art time can be totally unrelated to the theme. There are days when the teacher plans an art project that he/she considers important because of the final product. However, for the child it is important that the teacher plans art for art's sake.

Project Guidelines

Here are some guidelines to follow when developing and carrying out art project plans.

- The most important thing to remember is that the process a child goes through while making the art is key, not how the product looks when completed.
- Projects planned should be appropriate to the developmental age group of the children.
- Projects should be able to be completed in approximately 20 minutes.
- All tools should be safe to use unassisted and should be child-sized.
- Monitor the number of children at the art area so that it does not become overwhelming.
- Art is in the eye of the beholder. A dog can be purple and the cow can be green. Sometimes "we just like it that way."
- Set up the materials in advance. There is nothing that will cause disruption in the classroom quite so much as children waiting for a project to be prepared.
- Art time should occur on a daily basis.
- Mediums and textures should be alternated.
- Choose projects that can be cleaned up with the help of the children.
- Accept the fact that art is messy.

Art Project Skills

When planning art activities, it is useful to keep in mind the skills that are enhanced through the use of various tools and mediums. These include the following:

- When children use paste and glue, they foster their imaginations and creativity. They also learn about textures. Creating patterns and designs helps to build pre-math skills.
- Being able to distinguishing patterns from a background is related to reading.
- When children cut with scissors, they learn to control the small muscles in their hands. They learn about the shape, size, and location of objects.
- When children paint on an easel, they develop eye-hand coordination and creativity. It helps them to express their feelings and ideas, teaching them that their ideas have value.

All About Art (cont.)

Art Project Skills *(cont.)*

- When children use finger paints, they express themselves. They mix colors to make new colors. The concepts of shape, size, and location are learned. Most of all, they find an acceptable way to make a mess.

- When children scribble and draw, they learn to control the pressure needed to make the marks they want. This helps to strengthen fingers and small muscles in the hand.

- Children can express themselves with words when describing their artwork.

Tools of the Trade

The great thing about art and young children is that almost anything can be used to create art. Here are some simple suggestions and how they can be used for preschool art.

Sponges: Use sponges of all sizes and shapes, although little hands work better with smaller sponges. Your local craft store will carry sponges for different holiday patterns and projects. You can easily cut up kitchen sponges in the shapes and sizes you desire.

To get a sponge-painting effect, pour a small amount of paint into a flat container. Have the child pat the sponge lightly in the paint and then "hop" the sponge from spot to spot. Be careful not to press or "squash" the sponge onto the paper. Too much paint will blot onto the paper and you will not get as much mileage out of the paint nor will you get the effect you wanted. This also keeps the paint from soaking through the paper.

Brushes: Brushes come in different widths, both in brush size and handle size. Experiment with different brushes, including toothbrushes, housepainting brushes, basting brushes, combs, and hairbrushes, too.

Crayons: Many people feel that little fingers need to use only big, fat, chunky crayons. However, to really work on pincer grasp and control when coloring, use small broken crayons and the slimmer crayons. When crayons become too small to use, peel the paper and put them aside. Use them for a color-blending project by melting them together.

Markers: Markers are a preferred marking tool for little ones. This is because it does not take a lot of force to make a mark on the paper. This is an immediate reinforcement for those whose upper extremities are on the weaker side. Taking caps off and putting caps on the markers is a great eye-hand coordination activity, also.

Stamps and Stamp Pads: Be sure to purchase washable stamp pads, and make sure everyone is wearing a smock for this activity. Most ink from stamp pads is not washable and will stain clothing. Your local craft store will have a supply of seasonal or theme-oriented stamps.

Paint: Paint comes in many varieties. Tempera paint generally comes in a small or large bottle. It can come dry or in liquid form. It is generally washable, but if you put a little dish soap in the paint as you pour it in a spill-proof container and stir, it will wash out easier. Finger paint comes already made and is very thick. Finger-paint paper is best for this type of paint. Just remember that a little goes a long way.

All About Art (cont.)

Tools of the Trade *(cont.)*

Glue: Glue now comes in many colors and varieties. Choose the glue you need specific to the activity. If the younger child needs to glue, please give him/her some assistance or use a glue stick. When children are left to their own and are not "experienced" gluers, they make the nicest puddles of glue on their paper. These puddles seems to take forever to dry and will drip over the entire paper and floor if lifted upright. A glue stick is quick and much less messy. To prevent the glue puddles, pour a small amount of glue onto a piece of aluminum foil and let them use a cotton swab to dab the glue and "draw" it where it needs to be. This helps the children to be independent.

Clothesline: Retractable clotheslines are a wonderful way to help art projects dry out of the way of little hands. Attach one side to a wall and a hook to the opposite wall; pull open when you need it. When you are finished, just one pull and it is out of your way.

Bingo Markers: Bingo markers are great for little fists that just like to mark. This is also a useful cause-effect tool.

Foods: Pudding and gelatin are great in the powdered form or in the liquid form; there are a variety of colors, smells, and tastes. Be sure to watch out for the freshness of the foods used. Some last a long time and some do not.

Food Coloring: This is the best way to make tints in things you are using. A few drops usually does it. One box should last a whole year.

Classroom Supply List

Here is a list of supplies to keep handy for art projects.

- paper
- newsprint
- scrap paper
- tagboard
- finger paint
- play dough
- markers (fat and skinny)
- glitter
- craft sticks
- yarn
- fabric
- sponges
- clothespins
- paintbrushes
- smocks and shirts to cover clothing
- construction paper
- finger-paint paper
- scissors (adult and child)
- ink pads and stamps
- tempera paint (liquid and powder)
- crayons (large and small)
- chalk (colored, white, and large sidewalk chalk)
- glue (sticks, gel, school glue, and colored glue)
- paste
- tape (masking and cellophane; colored masking tape)
- wallpaper books
- clothesline
- watercolors
- no-spill paint cups

Letter to Parents About Art Supplies

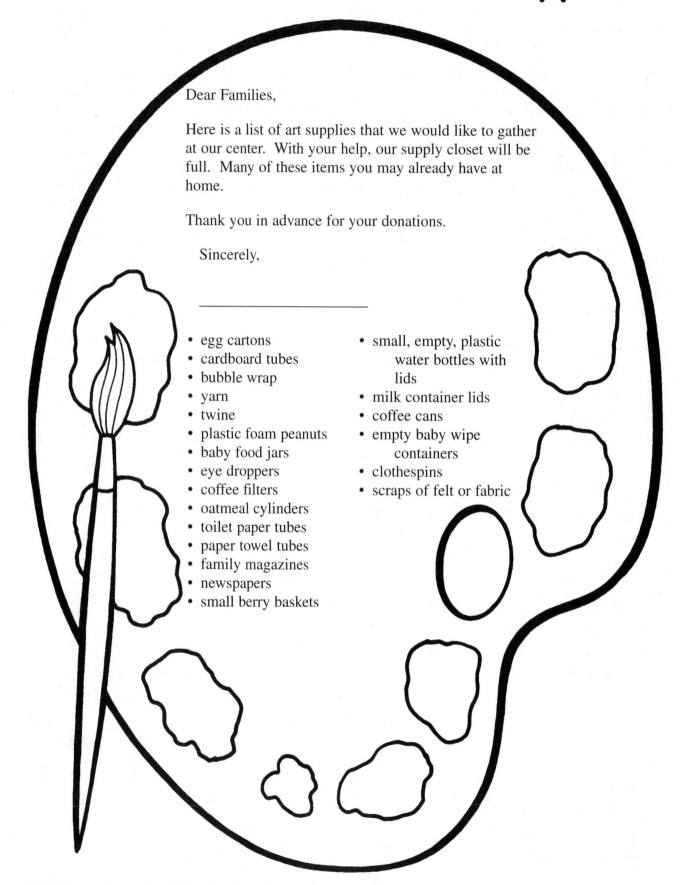

Dear Families,

Here is a list of art supplies that we would like to gather at our center. With your help, our supply closet will be full. Many of these items you may already have at home.

Thank you in advance for your donations.

Sincerely,

_____

- egg cartons
- cardboard tubes
- bubble wrap
- yarn
- twine
- plastic foam peanuts
- baby food jars
- eye droppers
- coffee filters
- oatmeal cylinders
- toilet paper tubes
- paper towel tubes
- family magazines
- newspapers
- small berry baskets

- small, empty, plastic water bottles with lids
- milk container lids
- coffee cans
- empty baby wipe containers
- clothespins
- scraps of felt or fabric

Free Art Supplies

There are a variety of sources for acquiring free art supplies. Here are a few of the most prominent.

After the winter holidays, many of the major **greeting card stores** want unsold holiday cards shipped back to their headquarters, but they do not want the envelopes. The store clerks in charge of the card department may be willing to save the envelopes for your use.

Ask **parents** to donate used computer paper from their homes or offices.

Use the letter provided (page 180) to ask parents to donate some of the things you need.

Newspaper offices often have leftover ends of plain newsprint for free or a nominal fee. Most rolls are 20–25 feet (6–8.5 m) long and are wide enough for large murals, body tracings, or making giant picture books.

Lumber and hardware stores usually have small pieces of wood scraps in various shapes and sizes they give away. Just bring a box with you to carry the scraps.

Paint stores offer free, outdated wallpaper sample books. These make great book covers and cards.

Printing shops have a steady supply of scraps available in various shapes, colors, and textures. Most printers are glad to collect the scraps for you.

Upholstery shops or custom fabric stores have out-of-date fabric samples they will give away. Use them for collages, texture books, or other projects.

More Ideas

There are many ideas in this section of the book, and they are sure to inspire ideas of your own. Use this form to jot down your notes and the helpful ideas you hear from your colleagues.

My Art Project Ideas

Everyone has music inside,

So let a song ring out.

Just let it come right from your heart,

That's what it's all about.

—Greg Scelsea and David Kirschner

All About Music

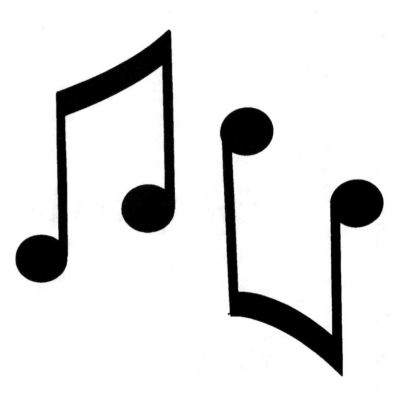

Music plays an important role in the lives of young children. Babies are rocked to sleep with lullabies. A toddler's constant motion is often accompanied by songs and chants of his or her own creation. Preschoolers enjoy creating their own soundmakers and are fascinated with the sounds they make with them.

Music includes singing, moving, listening, playing instruments, and creating music. Songs foster language development, social skills, rhythm, coordination, listening skills, and they are used as an outlet for feelings and ideas.

Music improves auditory discrimination, voice quality, memory, and sequencing skills, and it increases vocabulary while allowing the child to be an active learner. It can be used to teach many concepts and skills, including math, phonics, colors, shapes, feelings, and language concepts such as fast and slow, high and low, loud and soft, and more. Music also helps children to interpret and understand signals and cues they hear.

Researchers are finding that music can boost the brain power of children. They have discovered that when young children are exposed to singing, playing instruments, and listening to classical or other complex music, they have higher spatial and temporal intelligence test scores and their ability for mathematical reasoning is increased. Classical music helps to develop speech, movement abilities, and left-brain thinking skills.

"The Mozart Effect"

Dr. Alfred Tomatis, a French physician, believes that Mozart's music prepares the mind and body for learning, creativity, and rest. He asserts that even in the womb (after five months), babies are aware of high sound frequencies. Certain melodies (frequencies) help to stimulate the language centers of the brain, and the music by Mozart gives the healthiest of sounds. Mozart's music is simple, clear, organized, efficient, not overly emotional, and it is easy to listen to while being relaxing and inspiring. He recommends playing Mozart in the classroom as background music, emphasizing never to play the music too loudly and no longer than 25 minutes at a time. (Anything over 25 minutes reduces the effectiveness of the music.) You can read more about Mozart's music in Don Campbell's book *The Mozart Effect*.

Musical Instruments and Aids

Following is a list of instruments and sound makers as well as directions for making them. All of these are worthwhile to have in a preschool classroom.

Instruments and Aids

- records, tapes, and compact discs
- record, tape, and/or compact disc players
- songbooks
- song cards (page 186)
- fingerplays

- chants
- instruments: rhythm sticks, shakers, tambourines, and maracas (below); kazoos, drums, and hummer flutes (page 186)

Rhythm Sticks

Materials: paper bags and tape

Directions: Take a paper bag and roll it into a tight cylinder. Tape securely. Use these sticks to pound on cardboard blocks or furniture to make drumming sounds.

Shakers

Materials: uncooked rice or beans; paper cups, small or large plates, or lunch bags; tape

Directions: Put rice or beans inside two cups or plates tightly taped at the rim or inside a lunch bag taped shut. Shake.

Tambourines

Materials: two paper plates or foil pans for each child, crayons, dried beans, masking tape or glue

Directions: Decorate the plates or pie tins with the crayons. Put a handful of beans onto the plate. Lay the other plate over the top of the first plate, and tape around the sides so that the beans will not fall out. Shake and bang to music.

Maracas

Materials: small juice cans or cardboard tubes, tinfoil, dried macaroni, rubber bands, ribbons or crepe paper (optional)

Directions: Cover one end of the tube with foil or construction paper. Secure this with a rubber band. Fill the tube with dried macaroni. Cover the end as before. Decorate with ribbon or crepe paper streamers if desired.

Musical Instruments and Aids (cont.)

Comb Kazoos

Materials: combs, waxed paper or tissue paper

Directions: Fold the paper in half and wrap the teeth of the comb over the fold. Put your lips over the fold and hum a tune, moving the comb from side to side. Throw away the paper after each use and rinse the comb in warm water and antibacterial soap.

Drums

Materials: empty coffee cans or oatmeal cartons with plastic lids; masking tape; spoons; unsharpened pencils with erasers, or sticks; paper; crayons; glue; glitter; yarn or string

Directions: Glue the lid to the can or carton. Decorate paper with crayons, glue, and glitter to cover the can. Affix with tape or yarn/string. Cut a piece of yarn or string to the necessary length that will allow the drum to hang comfortably around the child's neck. (Be cautious, never allowing the children to play with these alone. The strings around their necks could be dangerous if left unattended.) Use a stick or pencil for a drumstick.

Hummer Flutes

Materials: cardboard tubes from paper towel or toilet paper rolls, tissue paper, rubber bands, pencils

Directions: Use the pencil to punch three or four holes in the tube. Cover one end of the tube with a small piece of tissue and secure it with tape or the rubber band. Hum a tune in the end without the paper and put your fingers over the holes.

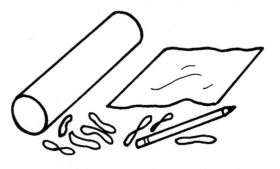

Song Cards

Materials: paper, writing instrument, songbooks, laminator (if available)

Directions: Make one card for each song. Write the words on the card and draw a corresponding illustration. This allows the nonverbal or young child to pick a song he or she enjoys by identifying a picture. The size of the card can vary for each setting. These cards are especially helpful for substitute teachers since they will know at a glance the songs the children enjoy as well as the words to the songs.

Here is a card example. To make a card for "The Wheels on the Bus," trace a picture of a bus on one side of the card. On the reverse side, print the words to the song.

Songs and Chants

Here are a number of simple song and chant ideas the children will enjoy.

Nursery Songs

Sing any of the following nursery rhymes to the tune of "Ninety-Nine Bottles of Beer on the Wall."

- Hey Diddle Diddle
- Jack and Jill
- Little Bo Peep
- Old Mother Hubbard

- Hickory Dickory Dock
- Little Boy Blue
- Little Miss Muffet
- Peter, Peter, Pumpkin Eater

- Humpty Dumpty
- Little Jack Horner
- Old King Cole
- Mary, Mary, Quite Contrary

Songs for Fun

The Ants Go Marching
(tune: "When Johnny Comes Marching Home")

The ants go marching one by one,
Hurrah, hurrah!
The ants go marching one by one,
Hurrah, hurrah!
The ants go marching one by one,
The little one stops to suck his thumb,
And they all go marching down in the ground
To get out of the rain,
Boom! Boom! Boom!

Two, tie his shoe.
Three, climb a tree.
Four, shut the door.
Five, take a dive.
Six, pick up sticks.
Seven, wave to heaven.
Eight, shut the gate
Nine, check the time.
Ten, say, "The end."

Body Parts
(tune: "Row, Row, Row Your Boat")

Head, arms, finger, hands,
Shoulders, knees and toes.
Eyes, ears, nose and mouth,
A healthy body grows.

Can You Do This?
(tune: "Are You Sleeping?")

Can you do this? Can you do this?
Look at me. Look at me.
Everybody try it, everybody try it.
You will see. You will see.

Songs and Chants (cont.)

Traditional Songs

Three Little Ducks

Three little ducks went out to play
Over the hills and far away.
Mama Duck called them, "Quack, quack, quack."
Two little ducks came running back.
Two little ducks went out to play
Over the hills and far away.
Mama Duck called them, "Quack, quack, quack."
One little duck came running back.
One little duck went out to play
Over the hills and far away.
Mama Duck called them, "Quack, quack, quack."
No little ducks came running back.
Papa Duck called them, "Quack, quack, quack."
Three little ducks came running back.

The Wheels on the Bus

The wheels on the bus go 'round and 'round,
'Round and 'round, 'round and 'round,
The wheels on the bus go 'round and 'round,
All over town.
The people on the bus go up and down . . .
The wipers on the bus go swish, swish, swish . . .
The horn on the bus goes beep, beep, beep . . .
The lights on the bus go blink, blink, blink . . .
The door on the bus goes open and shut . . .
The money on the bus goes clink, clink, clink . . .
The driver on the bus goes "Move on back," . . .
The baby on the bus goes "Wah! wah! wah!" . . .
The mommy on the bus goes "Sh! sh! sh!" . . .
The kids on the bus go "Yak! yak! yak!" . . .

*(Note: Alter the song to fit other units. For example,
"The cow on the farm says 'Moo, moo, moo,'" or,
"The drum in the band goes boom, boom, boom.")*

Eensy Weensy Spider

The eensy, weensy spider went up the water spout.
Down came the rain and washed the spider out.
Up came the sun and dried up all the rain,
And the eensy weensy spider went up the spout again.

Songs and Chants (cont.)

Traditional Songs *(cont.)*

I Have a Little Turtle

I have a little turtle.
His name is Tiny Tim.
I put him in the bathtub
To see if he could swim.
He drank up all the water,
He ate up all the soap.
He woke up in the morning
With bubbles in his throat:
Glug, glug, glug, glug.

Finger Family

Tommy Thumb is up,
And Tommy Thumb is down.
Tommy Thumb is dancing
All around the town.
Dance him on your shoulder,
Dance him on your head,
Dance him on your knee,
And tuck him into bed.

(Note: You can change the body parts as desired.)

Hands Up

Reach for the ceiling, touch the floor.
Stand up again, let's do more.
Touch your head, then your knees.
Go to your shoulder like this. See?
Reach for the ceiling, touch the floor.
That's all now. There isn't any more.

Name Chant

Names are short.
Names are long.
Say your name,
And clap along.

(Say name and clap the syllables.)

Songs and Chants (cont.)

Good-bye Songs

Good-bye Child
(tune: "Where Is Thumbkin?")
Good-bye (child's name).
Good-bye (child's name).
We like you.
Yes we do.
Good-bye (child's name).
Good-bye (child's name).
We like you.
 Yes we do.
(Note: For "child's name," insert one, two, or four names, depending on the group size.)

Good-bye, Child
(tune: "Goodnight Ladies")
Good-bye, (child's name).
Good-bye, (child's name).
Good-bye, (child's name).
I'm so glad you came (or "It's time for us to go.")

Clap Your Hands and Wiggle Your Toes
(tune: "Twinkle, Twinkle, Little Star")
Clap your hands and wiggle your toes,
That's the way this silly song goes.
Wink one eye, lift hands high,
Now it's time to say, "Good-bye."

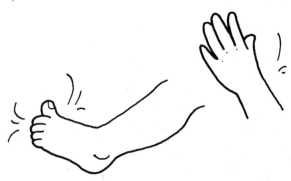

Gathering Songs

Gathering Song
(tune: "Skip to My Lou")
Come, come sit on a chair.
Come, come sit on a chair.
Come, come sit on a chair.
Sit on a chair and sing.
(Can also sing, "Sit on the mat/floor/etc.")

Clap, clap, clap your hands.
Clap, clap, clap your hands.
Clap, clap, clap your hands.
Clap your hands and sing.

Touch, touch, touch your nose.
Touch, touch, touch your nose.
Touch, touch, touch your nose.
Touch your nose with me.

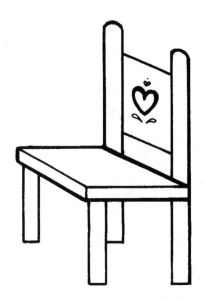

Songs and Chants (cont.)

Gathering Songs *(cont.)*

If You're Ready

(tune: "If You're Happy and You Know It")

If you're ready for your snack say, "Let's eat."
If you're ready for your snack say, "Let's eat."
If you're ready for your snack,
If you're ready for your snack,
If you're ready for your snack say, "Let's eat."

(Note: Alternatively sing, "If you're ready to go outside/to go play/to sing songs/etc." Also sing "cock-a-doodle-doo," "ah-choo," "boo" [for Halloween], "jingle bells" [for Christmas], "I love you" [for Valentine's Day], or an animal sound such as oink-oink in place of "Let's eat.")

All Around the Room

(tune: "All Around the Mulberry Bush")

All around the room I looked,
I couldn't find *(child's name)*.
I think I'll look in the chair,
Oops, there is *(child's name)*.

Group Songs

We're Sitting All Together

(tune: "The More We Get Together")

We're sitting all together, together, together.
We're sitting all together as happy as can be.
There's *(child's name)* and *(child's name)* and *(child's name)* and *(child's name)*.
We're sitting all together as happy as can be.

He Wore His Striped Shirt

(tune: "Mary Wore Her Red Dress")

(Child's name) wore her/his striped shirt,
Striped shirt, striped shirt.
(Child's name) wore her/his striped shirt
To school today.

Here We Are Together

(tune: "The More We Get Together")

Here we are together, together, together.
Here we are together.
We're having so much fun.
There's *(child's name)* and *(child's name)* and *(child's name)* and *(child's name)*.
Here we are together.
We're having such fun.

Songs and Chants (cont.)

Group Songs *(cont.)*

You Are a Girl/Boy

(tune: "The Farmer in the Dell")

(Child's name) is a girl/boy.
(Child's name) is a girl/boy.
(Child's name) is a g-i-r-l/b-o-y
(Child's name) is a girl/boy.
(**Note:** At the third line, hold out the girl or boy.)

I Stretch My Hands Up High

(tune: "The Farmer in the Dell")

I stretch my hands up high.
I stretch my hands up high.
I stretch up high to reach the sky.
I stretch my hands up high.
I put them in my lap.
I put them in my lap.
Now they are quiet as can be.
I put them in my lap.

Stand Up Tall

(chant)

Stand up tall,
Hands in the air.
Now sit down
In your chair.
Clap your hands
And make a frown,
Now make a big smile
Like a happy clown.

Come Gather Together

(tune: "For He's a Jolly Good Fellow")

Come, let's gather together,
Come, let's gather together,
Come, let's gather together,
To see what we can do *(share, plan, etc.)*.

Songs and Chants (cont.)

Group Songs *(cont.)*

Down the Hall
(tune: "This Is the Way We Wash Our Clothes")

Here we go walking down the hall,
Down the hall, down the hall.
Here we go walking down the hall
On our way outside.
(Note: You can substitute marching, skipping, or hopping on your way to music, art, etc.)

Transition Songs

Time to Clean Up
(tune: "The Muffin Man")

Oh, do you know what time it is,
What time it is, what time it is?
Oh, do you know what time it is?
It's time to clean up.

Clean-up Time Is Here
(tune: "London Bridge")

Clean-up time is already here,
Already here, already here.
Clean-up time is already here,
Watch us as we clean.

A Helper I Will Be
(tune: "The Farmer in the Dell")

A helper I will be.
A helper I will be.
I'll pick up my things and put them away.
A helper I will be.

This Is the Way We Clean Our Room
(tune: "This Is the Way We Wash Our Clothes")

This is the way we clean our room,
Clean our room, clean our room,
This is the way we clean our room,
Each and every day.

We're Cleaning Up Our Room
(tune: "The Farmer in the Dell")

We're cleaning up our room.
We're cleaning up our room.
We're putting everything away.
We're cleaning up our room.

Songs and Chants (cont.)

Transition Songs (*cont.*)

Oh, It's Clean-up Time
(*tune: "Clementine"*)

Oh, it's clean-up,
Oh, it's clean-up,
Oh, it's clean-up time right now.
It is time to put the toys away.
It's clean-up time right now.
(*Note: Also substitute "toys"*
for blocks, puzzles, etc.)

Time to Put the Toys Away
(*tune: "Mary Had a Little Lamb"*)

It's time to put the toys away,
Toys away, toys away,
It's time to put the toys away
So we can go to play.
(*Note: Also substitute other activities for which to prepare.*)

Clean Up
(*chant*)

Clean up, clean up
Everybody, everywhere.
Clean up, clean up,
Everybody do your share.

Clean Up Song
(*tune: "Twinkle, Twinkle, Little Star"*)

Twinkle, twinkle, little star,
Time to clean up where you are.
Put a toy back in its place,
Keep a smile on your face,
Twinkle, twinkle, little star,
Time to clean up where you are.

More Ideas

There are many ideas in this section of the book, and they are sure to inspire ideas of your own. Use this form to jot down your notes and the useful ideas you hear from your colleagues.

My Music Ideas and Song Lyrics

The important thing is not to stop questioning.

—*Albert Einstein*

All About Circle Time

Circle time is the time set aside in the schedule for the teacher and class to interact positively as a group. This is where the theme will be presented and where good language and cognitive activities are planned and acted upon. In circle time, the children are allowed to communicate ideas to the group and to receive a response. Children see their efforts as being important and their self worth is fostered. Circle time provides a place in which language and cognitive and social skills can all develop in a natural way.

Young children attend to the task at hand. Teachers must be structured yet flexible with their plans. Information presented to young children must be useful and part of "their world." Children learn by exploring, so lessons must be planned that use all the child's senses: taste, sight, sound, touch, and smell. The child will then learn to use these senses to integrate the new information presented.

Pre-Academics

Circle time is the one large-group activity in the day in which pre-academics are presented. These include a wide range of concept-building activities. Here is a list of things to include:

- how things are labeled
- how things are described (color, shape, size, length, quantity, weight, feel, and sound)
- properties of objects (how things fit together, their compositions, their uses)
- similarities and differences
- sequencing
- cause and effect
- families
- schools
- communities
- plants and animals
- the atmosphere
- ecology
- natural processes
- learning how to question
- learning how to discover
- learning how to reason

The Teacher as Guide

The role of the preschool teacher in circle time is that of a guide. The teacher will guide the children through the lesson, encouraging language and thinking skills while fostering good social and turn-taking skills. This can all be done through developmentally-appropriate activities. The teacher will help to build the child from the inside out and to encourage the growth and development of the next generation. All of this happens in less than 30 minutes a day!

All About Circle Time (cont.)

Setting Up Circle Time

Set aside a quiet section of the room that will be without distraction. Locate the following items:

- bulletin board, flannelboard or magnetic board
- tape player or record player
- apron with pockets
- box for prop items or display items
- table
- proper seating for children to eliminate distractions and promote good posture

Transitions to Circle Time

An easy way to let the children know that the transition to circle time has begun is to sing a transition song. (See pages 193–194.)

Once the children are seated begin your circle time with a standard activity ritual that you will use every day. While flexibility is essential, structure and "sameness" are crucial. The teacher must find a balance of each. Here are a few activities to use to begin circle time.

- Count the boys and girls in the group. Display the numbers. Ask which number is larger.
- Ask everyone to say his or her name. Older children can say their whole name while younger children can identify themselves from a picture.
- Play "Who's Missing?" Ask the children to look around the group to see who is missing. Pass out the children's pictures to them. After all the pictures are passed out, talk about the child's picture that is remaining.
- If any of the children are absent from the group, ask the "why" and "where" questions. For example, "Why isn't Jose in school today?" and "Where do you think Jose might be?" Accept all answers and invite discussion on what happened when these children were last sick or went on a trip.
- Ask who in the group has news. Write the news on a blackboard. Set it aside for the news of the day. Allow time for each child to say something.
- Introduce the concept or activity.
- Do calendar-type activities such as naming and labeling the day, week, month, and year. Calendar activities that ask children about the day, month, or year are not appropriate for those students under the age of three. Choose another opening activity for them.
- Talk about the weather and ask questions such as: "How do I know it is cold outside?" "If it is hot outside, do I wear shorts or pants?" "How do I know I am wearing shorts?" and "Are my legs showing?"

All About Circle Time (cont.)

Presenting a Theme

Is there an order the teacher should use when planning a unit? The answer is yes. Ease planning woes by following the sequential steps presented here.

	Example: *"Yellow" Theme*
Day 1 Introduce a broad concept.	**Day 1:** When introducing the concept, begin with the basis for the concept. For example: "We have lots of colors in our world. Can you tell me some colors? Here is a beautiful color. It is yellow." Now talk about items that are yellow.
Day 2 Review the broad concept presented the day before and the negative or opposite (the "not") of the broad concept.	**Day 2:** The "nots" are important parts of the concept. They help children begin to understand some of the details of a concept. Review the basic concept and add to it the negative or opposite such as "This is yellow, and this is not yellow." Repetition and questioning of items work well here. Labeling the other color or detail is not necessary at this point. Do not ask whether the bus, for example, is yellow. State and ask, "This bus is yellow. Show me what is not yellow."
Day 3 Distinguish between concept and non-concept.	**Day 3:** This activity should allow the children to sort and distinguish the concept and non-concept. For example, say, "Let's put all the yellow blocks in this bucket and all the blocks that are not yellow in this bucket" (providing two different buckets).
Day 4 Use the concept in the children's environment.	**Day 4:** These activities include hunt and find, labeling, sorting, and cooking lessons.
Day 5 Generalize the concept.	**Day 5:** Activities on this day should include stories, fingerplays, creative projects, sharing, and using the concept in hands-on ways.

All About Circle Time (cont.)

Follow-up Activities

Once the teacher has finished the main activity and covered the "meat" of the theme for the day, it is time to use a follow-up activity to reinforce the concept. When choosing a reinforcing activity, involve the whole child with a movement, fine motor skill, or cooking activity.

For example, a fine motor follow-up for "yellow" might be for the children to place all yellow bears on yellow circles. For cooking, make lemonade from scratch, which also involves texture, size, shape, smell, measuring, and squeezing. A gross motor follow-up activity is to have the children step on yellow circles when the music stops.

Closure

The teacher must always have closure for any activity planned, but especially for a group activity such as circle time. This is the time to recapture their attention and to help transition this activity to the next one.

A good transition activity is to use a sequence of pictures to show what has happened in the day. Talk about what they have done, turning over the pictures as you do so. Talk about what is going to happen next and for the rest of the day. Leave the sequence cards available during free play so that the children can look at them and reinforce the daily sequence of events on their own.

After discussing the sequence, a good-bye song and self-affirmation hug (give yourself a big hug) helps to finish the activity, and these are obvious signs that another activity is about to begin. After the song, ask each child to "do something" before the next activity starts. This may mean anything from each child tossing a yellow beanbag into a bucket to each child placing his or her chair at the snack table before sitting down to a snack.

More Ideas

There are many ideas in this section of the book, and they are sure to inspire ideas of your own. Use this form to jot down your notes and the useful ideas you hear from your colleagues.

My Circle Time Ideas

Where there is an inquisitive mind there will always be a frontier.

—*Anonymous*

All About Field Trips

Field trips are the perfect way to teach children about the world around them. Each community can be turned into a classroom. Field trips teach children many things, whether they are just around the corner or in an exciting destination at the end of a bus ride. They help children to develop observation skills. Children use their senses while exploring, and they see, smell, taste, touch, and listen to the things around them to gain new information about their world and themselves. First-hand experiences are always better than pictures that are only two dimensional.

Field trips help children to expand their understanding of what people do. They discover similarities and differences among workers in their community. Children use the information and incorporate it into their play.

Field trips help children to reinforce what they already know. They are dynamic ways to increase vocabulary and to create excitement in learning, becoming springboards for future topics. Depending on the age and abilities of your children, introduce where the class will be going and what they can expect to see.

Transportation can be arranged in many ways. Parents can drive if they have proof of insurance (which should be on file at the school prior to any excursion). School buses may also be used, or perhaps there are organizations in your area that offer buses for nonprofit organizations.

During the field trips, there are so many concepts that can be pointed out and discussed. Colors, sizes, shapes, quantity, feel, smell, taste, and language can be developed, and the children can put their behavior and social skills to use.

It is always a good idea to take a camera for pictures to be used after the children have returned. With the developed pictures back in class, discuss the trip. Let the children tell you what they saw and did. They might also draw pictures of what they did and then sequence them in the order that they happened.

The children can be encouraged to act out the experience. For example, if you visited a fire station, let the children reenact what firefighters do. Another activity is to make a collage or a book. The children can sequence the photos of the trip and then dictate captions to include in the book. Parents also enjoy the photos to share with their children, which is particularly valued by those parents who were unable to participate in the trip.

Community Resources

The community is full of exciting places to visit. The best trips are those in which the children are interested. If they are studying foods, then a trip to the supermarket, a bakery, or a restaurant will be rewarding. Sometimes going on a field trip before a unit of study gives the children a point of reference they may not have had previously. Here are some places that make for ideal field trips.

- airport
- animal shelter
- bakery
- bookstore
- car dealer
- city hall
- coffee/donut shop
- college campus
- construction site
- dairy
- deli
- department store
- doctor/dentist office
- eye-care store
- fabric store
- factory
- farm
- fire station
- florist

- fruit/vegetable stand
- garden center
- grocery store
- hairdresser
- hardware store
- ice cream store
- library
- pet store
- pizzeria
- police station
- post office
- radio/television station
- school building
- shoe repair shop
- shoe store
- shopping mall
- toy store
- veterinarian's office

A good source for ideas is to survey parents at the beginning of the year, asking where they would like their child to visit and if they might host a visit themselves, sharing their jobs or workplaces with the class.

On any trip you take, be sure to bring your emergency bag (page 36) complete with emergency forms (page 49) and permission slips (page 206).

Field Trip Organizing Roster

Destination: _____

Date: _____

Name	Permission received?	Money received?	Parent driving?	Number of passengers

Teacher Note: Attach this form to a manila clasp envelope and put the returned permission slips and money inside. This will provide you with a quick reference for all pertinent information.

Permission Slip

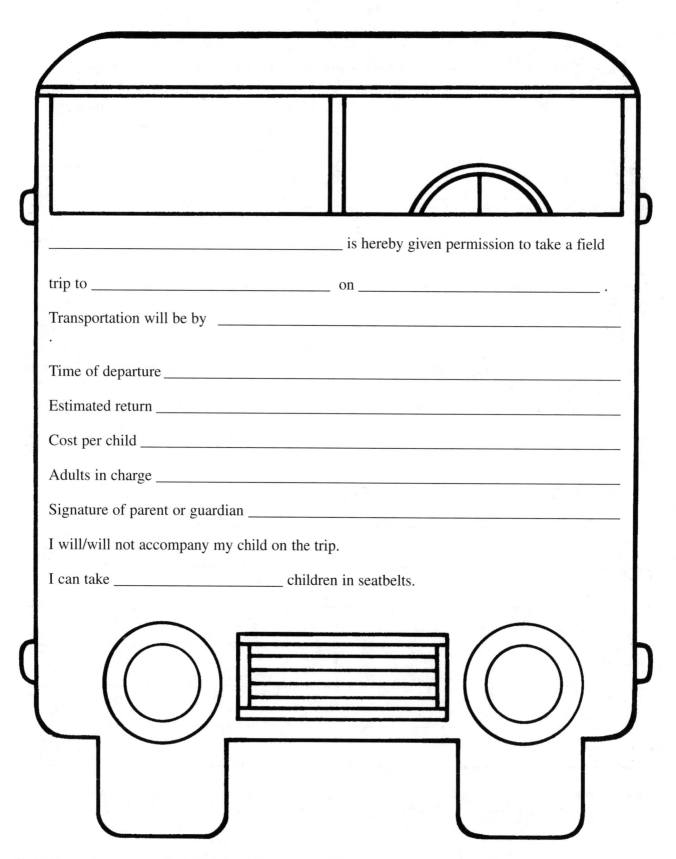

_____ is hereby given permission to take a field

trip to _____ on _____ .

Transportation will be by _____
.

Time of departure _____

Estimated return _____

Cost per child _____

Adults in charge _____

Signature of parent or guardian _____

I will/will not accompany my child on the trip.

I can take _____ children in seatbelts.

"Walking" Trip Permission Slip

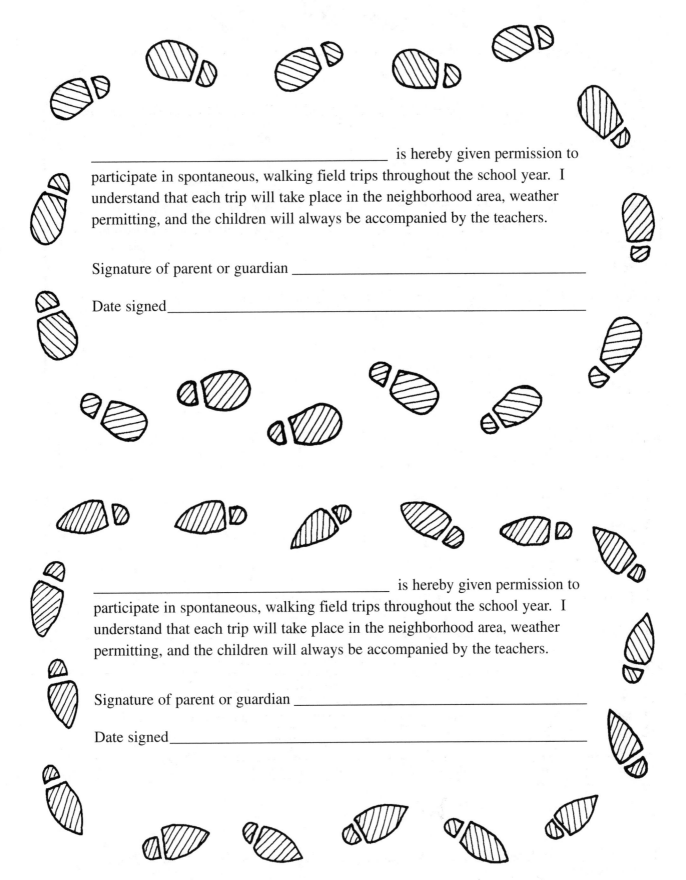

_____ is hereby given permission to participate in spontaneous, walking field trips throughout the school year. I understand that each trip will take place in the neighborhood area, weather permitting, and the children will always be accompanied by the teachers.

Signature of parent or guardian _____

Date signed_____

_____ is hereby given permission to participate in spontaneous, walking field trips throughout the school year. I understand that each trip will take place in the neighborhood area, weather permitting, and the children will always be accompanied by the teachers.

Signature of parent or guardian _____

Date signed_____

Statement of Insurance on Private Vehicles

School name _____

Address _____

Phone number _____ Fax number _____

School year _____

The above-named school/center requires proof of insurance in force on all private vehicles, prior to and during their use for the transportation of school sponsored trips on all in-county and out-of-county trips. The groups being transported include, but are not limited to, students, parents, teachers, staff, and volunteers.

This form is to be completed for each private vehicle used and is valid for the school year in which it is filed. If the insurance policy expires or is cancelled during the school year, a new statement must be submitted.

Date_____ Driver's name _____

Age _____ Driver's License number _____

This is to certify that insurance policies, subject to their terms, conditions and exclusions, are at present in force with the company indicated.

Name of insured _____

Policy number_____

Insurance company _____

Vehicle make _____ Year _____ Model_____

Policy period from _____ to _____

Identification number _____

This also certifies that the same provides for personal injury protection in a sum of not less than $10,000.00.

A photocopy of your insurance card and driver's license is required.

I certify that the above information is correct.

Signature of insured _____ Date signed _____

More Ideas

There are many ideas in this section of the book, and they are sure to inspire ideas of your own. Use this form to jot down your ideas and all pertinent information regarding field trip resources in your area.

My Field Trip Ideas, Addresses, Phone Numbers, and Contacts

Good discipline is a series of little victories in which a teacher, through small decencies, reaches a child's heart.

—*Haim Ginott*

All About Behavior

Positive Learning Environment

Every parent wants his or her child to be the best-behaved child in class. Every teacher hopes that this is true and that there will be no behavior problems in the class. Unfortunately, there are such problems from time to time. The purpose of this chapter is not to focus on the negativity of behavior problems but to help the teacher to establish a positive learning environment that is inviting to adults and children alike.

Establishing a positive environment in the classroom is important because such surroundings are the places where children learn best. They learn to respect themselves and one another, and their self concepts are enhanced. When the environment supports it, children learn to believe in themselves and their abilities to learn.

When a positive learning environment is established, the teacher creates a circle of success. Through individualized and group instruction, each child is surrounded by successful experiences. Each success, however small, supports increased efforts. Trying harder leads to success. A child becomes successful through success, not failure.

A teacher who sets up the classroom as a positive learning environment will find his or her job much easier. Children who like to learn and like being in the classroom are more enjoyable to teach. These children learn more, learn quicker, and with less teacher intervention regarding their behavior.

When regarding children's behavior, people often refer to it in terms of discipline problems. Discipline, quite simply, is the following of rules. If the teacher creates a positive set of rules for the class, discipline will not be a problem. Teaching and learning will become a joy!

These are the five general steps for setting up a positive learning environment.

1. **Rules:** Carefully determine the classroom rules based on the developmental age of the children being taught. For example, rules for twos should include "Share your toys," and a good rule for threes may be "When finished with a toy, put it on a shelf." Post the rules in the classroom. In a kind voice, verbally remind the children of the rules on a daily basis and at the beginning of each new activity.

2. **Approval:** Reward each child who is on task with praise. Praise does two things. It keeps a child on task and it enhances a child's self-concept. Praise often, using such phrases as, "I like the way you . . . " or "Great sharing!" Offer praise in a sincere voice, or it will not be effective. Praise for both effort and success.

3. **Ignoring:** It is best to ignore inappropriate behavior whenever possible. You can ignore a child who breaks class rules. When you refuse to give your attention to a child, he/she will stop that behavior and do something else to get your attention. When inappropriate behavior is not rewarded, it will stop. You may have to wait for a temporary increase in the misbehavior. This is a testing phase. Be patient and wait it out.

All About Behavior (cont.)

Positive Learning Environment *(cont.)*

4. **Disapproval:** Be negative only when necessary to stop an inappropriate behavior. The teacher must decide when misbehavior can no longer be ignored. You must stop behavior when a child can be hurt, when furnishings or materials may be destroyed, or when learning situations are being interrupted. The positive behavior must be rewarded three times after the negative is overcome.

5. **Redirection:** Redirection is the process of distracting and removing the negative action, turning to a positive action without reward or disapproval. An example of this is when two children are both pulling on a toy car, wanting to play with it. The teacher intervenes and gives one of the children another car. The children stop arguing about the toy and go about their play.

Consistency is its own reward. Children bloom in a positive learning environment. They relate freely with their friends and their teacher. They learn to treat each other positively. This, too, can be taught and rewarded by the teacher. (A variety of behavior awards are provided on pages 221–224.)

When It's Just Not Working

When children do not respond to a positive environment, try the following:

1. Responses for extreme behavior problems:
   - Stop inappropriate behaviors with disapproval that is strong enough to stop the behavior.
   - After 30 seconds, lavishly praise appropriate behavior.
   - Catch the child on task and continue to praise. This child needs positive reinforcement.
   - This child may need to be isolated from others in a "time-out" setting.

2. Responses to immaturity and a short attention span:
   - Use as much positive reinforcement as you can with this child.
   - Anticipate the attention span; praise before the child is in trouble.
   - Levels of attention will increase with the reinforcement of on-task behavior.
   - Be sure tasks are at a child's developmental level.

Use of Time Out

Time-out is a behavior modification tool that can be used successfully if applied in the correct situations. Oftentimes, it is used inappropriately. Check these guidelines.

- Never impose time-out on a child who is less than three years of developmental age; they do not understand the concept, and you will only increase everyone's frustration.

- Use only when all other methods of positive correction have been attempted.

- Place a chair away from the activity of others but in sight of all adults in the room.

- The golden rule for time-out is one minute for each year of the child's age plus one minute.

- Set a timer so that the child knows when the timer dings, his/her time is over.

- Afterwards, speak with the child to be sure he/she knows why there was a time-out.

- Praise the child immediately after the time-out for positive or on-task behavior.

Behavior Modification Parent Letter

Use this form to notify parents upon registration that certain behavior modification techniques such as time outs are used in the center for inappropriate behaviors. Always have the parents read and sign the form at registration, and keep the forms on file.

Center _____ Date _____

Child's name _____

Parent's name_____

Dear Families,

As part of our positive classroom environment, sometimes we encounter behaviors that are inappropriate for the classroom. These behaviors may include physical encounters between children, inappropriate language use, or failure to comply with classroom rules. Below is a list of the modifications that are utilized in this center and under which circumstances they are used.

Under no circumstances will corporal punishment (spanking, hitting) be imposed at this center.

Please sign at the bottom of this form, indicating that you have read and are aware of the techniques used at this center.

Behavior modification techniques used:

Parent signature _____ Date_____

The Angry Child

Dealing with the angry child is one of the toughest challenges a preschool teacher may face. Many times, routines can be interrupted by a child who is "losing it" by yelling, throwing things, or being aggressive towards others.

Remember that anger is not a bad emotion. It is an essential part of how a child learns and begins to understand the world. The feelings that accompany anger are competition and assertiveness. These are parts of what helps us to define who we are. Anger does not always come in the same form. Some angry children blow up due to emotional overload, some angry children have roots traced to frustration with motor problems, and some may need to let off steam in a reaction to the tensions in the home.

Your classroom may very well be the most stable place in a child's life. Here are some ways in which you can help a child to learn to control his or her anger.

1. Give this child some special attention during free play activity time. Get down on the floor and play with the child. Follow his/her lead. Give the child two rules in this play: He/she cannot hurt anyone or break anything.

2. Spend time solving problems together. Help the child to use his/her verbal abilities to anticipate the feelings that get him/her into a troubling situation. In this way, you are anticipating the situation before it happens and going over the correct behavior. You might add statements such as these to your activity transition: "Let's talk about going out to the playground. What happened yesterday with the sand bucket? Oh yes, Jose and Sam were fighting over the sand buckets. Today what do you think might happen? If you feel like hitting, what should you do instead?" You may have to keep this up for some time, but eventually the child can guide him/herself into the correct behavior.

3. Let the child know that you understand what he or she is feeling. You can say things like, "I understand that you want all the cars, but Taylor wants to play with the cars, too. What do you think we could do about that?"

4. Break down problems into small steps. This is a pick-your-battles kind of idea. If a child has several behaviors that need correcting, pick the behavior that is at the top of the list. Choose one behavior at a time and focus on extinguishing that first. Then focus on the next one on the list.

5. Set your limits. Be calm, positive, and friendly, but be firm and consistent.

Recognizing Clinical Hyperactivity

Our society is a quick-fix environment. The pace that families keep, the rapid activity with the computer age, and even fast food gives us the belief and desire that we can solve any problem in minutes. Hyperactivity is a problem associated with the inability to attend to academic activities. Hyperactivity is not just an academic problem—it is a life problem. More often than not, if the teacher is having problems with excessive activity or attention difficulties in the classroom, the parent has noticed some of these behaviors at home.

Teachers must be careful not to "diagnose" hyperactivity that is truly masking developmental problems. Here is a list of behaviors or patterns that may emerge with hyperactivity. If you see these consistently, speak to the parents in a private conference and show them the checklist provided. Ultimately, the child's pediatrician should address these concerns.

Common Behaviors of the Hyperactive Child

- constantly fidgets or squirms
- cannot stay seated
- is easily distracted
- cannot wait his/her turn
- blurts out things before questions are finished being asked
- does not follow instructions
- cannot play quietly
- talks excessively
- appears not to be listening
- interrupts other children's games or talk
- shifts from one activity to another, never finishing one
- cannot sustain work or play

Medical Factors Affecting Behavior

Not all children exhibiting the behaviors listed above are, in fact, hyperactive. Here is a list of other medical causes.

- metabolic conditions associated with low blood sugar
- thyroid abnormality
- medication used to treat chronic illnesses such as asthma
- urinary tract infection
- decreased hearing
- difficulties in understanding what is being said
- abnormality in brain function
- depression

Developmental Behaviors

The behaviors listed below may help the teacher to better understand the developmental behaviors that are appropriate for the age group being taught.

Typical 2½-Year-Old Behaviors

- ❏ demanding
- ❏ explosive emotions
- ❏ demand for sameness (order in the place occupied)
- ❏ bossy (because unsure)
- ❏ thumb sucking increases
- ❏ stuttering may appear temporarily
- ❏ temper tantrums
- ❏ frequent use of the word "no"
- ❏ extremes of emotions: exuberant to shy, independent to dependent
- ❏ does not share well
- ❏ frequent use of the word "why"
- ❏ very inquisitive
- ❏ easily exhausted (whining often an expression of this fatigue)
- ❏ easily frustrated
- ❏ interested in new things

Typical 3-Year-Old Behaviors

- ❏ plays nicely with other children; begins to interact with other children as they play
- ❏ not as self-centered as before (some ability to share)
- ❏ beginning to consider other children's feelings
- ❏ activity shifts rapidly (solitary play, adult interaction, aggressive co-play, cooperative play)
- ❏ gets along easily with others; conforming
- ❏ wants to please
- ❏ sure on his/her feet

Typical 3½-Year-Old Behaviors

- ❏ plays in groups of two, three, or more
- ❏ long, continuous, cooperative play
- ❏ imaginative play (dolls, building, etc.)
- ❏ interest and admiration for what others are doing
- ❏ friendships stronger and more intense than at three
- ❏ tendency to exclude children who are disliked or dissimilar
- ❏ interest in people increases over interest in objects
- ❏ wants own way
- ❏ emotionally insecure
- ❏ nonconforming; often refuses to obey
- ❏ inconsistency in emotions

Developmental Behaviors (cont.)

Typical 4-Year-Old Behaviors

- ❑ asks "why" frequently
- ❑ high energy
- ❑ vivid imagination
- ❑ constant motion
- ❑ does not like to do things twice
- ❑ biting nails
- ❑ exaggerated
- ❑ out-of-bounds (laughs and cries too much)
- ❑ vocabulary about 1,500 words

Typical 4½-Year-Old Behaviors

- ❑ interested in whether things are real
- ❑ more self-motivated than earlier
- ❑ highly emotional
- ❑ difficult to shift attention
- ❑ likes to make faces
- ❑ oppositional behavior
- ❑ unpredictable
- ❑ talkative
- ❑ constant motion
- ❑ fearful
- ❑ difficult to motivate
- ❑ likes to do familiar things
- ❑ likes to play dress-up
- ❑ enjoys rhymes and silly language
- ❑ appetite is only fair
- ❑ holds pencil with fist
- ❑ wobbly strokes with writing instrument
- ❑ paper is turned horizontally

Developmental Behaviors (cont.)

Typical 5-Year-Old Behaviors

- ❏ calm, collected, and self-contained
- ❏ becoming interested in the written word
- ❏ optimistic
- ❏ possessiveness
- ❏ meshes with the environment
- ❏ wants to be good
- ❏ close to mother
- ❏ quieter than before
- ❏ stomachaches are common
- ❏ good judge of what he/she can/cannot do
- ❏ does not worry
- ❏ responds well to praise
- ❏ usually eager to learn
- ❏ gets along well with peers
- ❏ two finger and thumb grip on pencil
- ❏ stays in seat more regularly
- ❏ sighs frequently

Typical 5½-Year-Old Behaviors

- ❏ oppositional behavior
- ❏ at odds with self and the environment
- ❏ ritualistic in nature
- ❏ nose picking, nail biting, and thumb sucking may increase
- ❏ sibling rivalry becomes dominant
- ❏ worrier
- ❏ hesitant, dawdling, and indecisive
- ❏ over-demanding and explosive
- ❏ emotions in a constant state of tension
- ❏ more susceptible to colds, headaches, earaches, and stomachaches
- ❏ less motor control than before
- ❏ awkward pencil grasp
- ❏ frequently loses visual orientation (reversals become common)

Talking to Children

Talking with children involves the exchange of words, ideas, and feelings. People communicate with their faces (smiles and frowns), with actions (hugs and gestures), and with words. Good communication leads to warm relationships, cooperation between others, and feelings of worth, all of which are the basis for a lifetime of success. Here are some ways to facilitate good communication.

- Use words that invite the child to say more such as "Tell me more" and "What else?"

- Listen attentively, pay attention, and get rid of distractions around you.

- Use messages that reflect the "you" in the child: "You are sad because the dog died" and "You are angry because you didn't win the game."

- Use "do" instead of "don't": "You can color on this page," not "Don't color on the table!"

- Talk with children and not at them. Be sure your conversations are two-sided.

- Use messages to communicate your thoughts: "I need help cleaning up the table."

- Make simple requests that are clear and easy to remember.

- Get the child's attention before speaking to him or her.

- Communicate at eye level. Adults forget that their size makes children feel small.

- Be polite. Say "please" and "thank you" to children, and they will return the favor.

- Do not use unkind words such as ridiculing, shaming, or namecalling.

- Use kind words to encourage and build up a child.

Self Check

Periodically it is beneficial to check yourself to be sure you are on track with the children. This is a good way to improve your teaching. Ask yourself the following questions.

Am I . . .

- being consistent?

- sticking with goals?

- accidentally reinforcing bad behavior through laughing, etc.?

- not using reinforcement often enough?

- using criticism, nagging, threats, and scolding?

- being pessimistic or positive?

- demanding verbal responses for everything the child wants (to encourage language)?

- using baby talk with children instead of adult speech?

- expecting an immediate change in behavior?

- letting the child control the environment?

Charting Children's Behaviors

When a child's behavior is particularly annoying to you or to one of the other children, and you are in the process of deciding what to do about it, you must first take a good look at the behavior. An easy and expeditious way to do this is to chart the behavior. This will give you a concrete picture of the behavior, how many times the behavior is demonstrated, and what might have caused the behavior.

Charting a behavior may seem to be out of your realm of experience, but it is not difficult. It is simple and easy to interpret. Choose the type of charting below that you feel is appropriate to the situation and follow the directions. This is a good tool to use for parent conferences if the behavior becomes a problem area.

Frequency Chart

This type of chart determines how many times the behavior is performed in any certain time frame. Teachers are very busy, so choose small amounts of time.

Behavior: hitting another child	**Child:** Susan	Date: 3-23-99
Time	**Activity**	**Frequency**
9:50–10:00	circle time	1
10:15–10:25	free play	5
11:30–11:40	cleanup	1
12:00–12:10	lunch	1

This chart shows that during the four time periods charted, Susan hit another child eight times. Five of those times however were during free play. This allows you to adjust your floor play time with Susan to help Susan become part of the positive environment you have arranged. It will also help you to decide which method of behavior modification you can use appropriately to turn the situation around and to extinguish the hitting behavior.

Duration Chart

This chart will help you to determine if the behavior is being performed for an unusual length of time. The basis for this chart is to show when the behavior begins and ends.

Behavior: crying		**Child:** Hector	**Date** 4-27-99
Time begins	**Time ends**	**Activity**	
8:17	8:27	parent leaves	
8:35	8:55	circle time	
9:15	9:30	snack ends; beginning free play	
10:00	10:20	clean up from free play; music time begins	

This chart indicates that Hector has trouble with transitions between activities. A warning to Hector to let him know what is coming next may be helpful so that the transition does not set him off into a crying spell. After you have noted this, the next thing you can do is to make a list of what works as a reinforcement for not crying. This may take awhile, but you are setting up good habits for a positive non-crying environment.

Behavior Awards

_____
child

Had a Super Day!

_____
teacher   date

_____
child

Had a BEEutiful Day!

_____
teacher   date

Behavior Awards (cont.)

_____
child

You Brighten My Day!

_____
teacher   date

_____
child

Had a Beary Special Day!

_____
teacher   date

Behavior Awards (cont.)

Glad-o-Gram

Couldn't wait to tell you . . .

_____
child

had a wonderful day!

_____
teacher   date

Just bubbling to tell you the news . . .

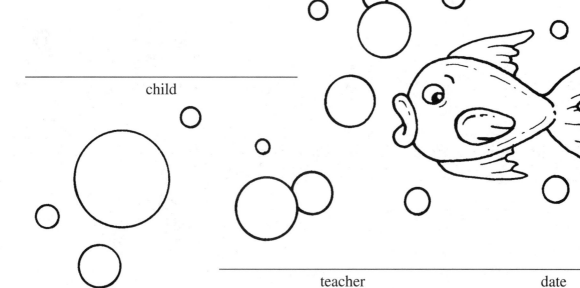

_____
child

_____
teacher   date

Behavior Awards (cont.)

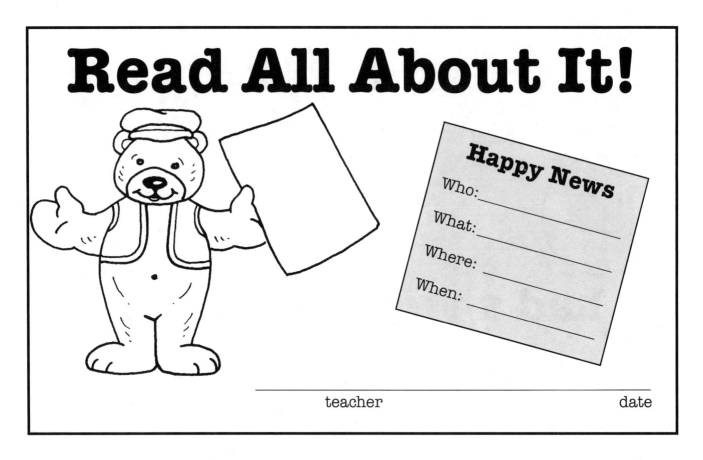

Read All About It!

Happy News

Who: _____

What: _____

Where: _____

When: _____

_____ _____
teacher   date

I Can Do It!

Today, _____
                        child

learned to_____
                            activity

We are so proud!

_____ _____
teacher   date

More Ideas

There are many ideas in this section of the book, and they are sure to inspire ideas of your own. Use this form to jot down your notes and the helpful ideas you hear from your colleagues.

My Behavioral Concerns, Support, and Contacts

In helping others, we shall help ourselves, for whatever good we give out completes the circle and comes back to us.

—Flora Edwards

All About Parent Conferences

Parent conferences can and should be rewarding experiences. A parent conference is a meeting between a child's parent(s) and teacher(s). The meeting brings out a good understanding of the child and his or her development. A parent conference is scheduled usually at the teacher's invitation, but sometimes parents ask for a conference. Conferences should be held at least twice a year.

There are several reasons for parent conferences. The first is progress. This means even though the children are preschoolers, there is a general rate of development at which children achieve. Some children learn at the "normal" rate, some exceed that, and others fall behind on the scale. There are also conferences to discuss behavior—these are general conferences just to touch base with the parent. The parent can report on such things as the child's attitudes, health, family relationships, interests, and any social factors that may come into play with the child's development. The teacher can report on such things as the child's attitude toward school and other children and progress in his or her development.

Here are a few ideas that will help the parent conference to go smoothly.

- ❏ **You will need comfortable, size-appropriate chairs.** If you sit in an adult chair and the only other chairs in the room are preschooler chairs, the parents will be sitting at an eye level below yours. That will increase tension and may make them feel intimidated and anxious.

- ❏ **You might begin your conference with an icebreaker such as refreshments of coffee and cookies and juice for the family.** This puts everyone at ease, and you begin on a positive note.

- ❏ **You should prepare yourself for the conference.** Make an outline of the points you would like to discuss. Collect work samples and documentation to show the parents. For example, if behavior is a problem and you can show the charting you have done (page 220), your point will be much better taken and understood.

- ❏ **You should always leave time at the end of the conference for questions from the parent.**

- ❏ **You should end your conference just as you began—on a positive note.** State some positive things about the child so that even a parent whose child is having trouble leaves with a warm sense of your concern and the child's worth.

Individual conferences are often preceded in the beginning of the year by an open house for the following purposes:

- to meet teachers
- to meet parents
- to tour the school and facilities
- to learn about the policies and standards of the center

Reproduce the forms on pages 229–230 to help your parent conferences go smoothly. Page 228 will help you to prepare for the conference, and page 231 should be completed at the time of registration.

Remember, communication is your best tool for a successful parent-teacher conference!

Parent Conference Checklist

Here is a list to help you plan a positive parent conference.

_____Make lists of what you want to tell the parent.

_____Begin with something positive.

_____Have samples of the child's work to support your observations.

_____Provide refreshments for the parents and children.

_____Set up the environment to respect the family's privacy.

_____Use adult furniture when possible.

_____Provide paper and pencils for note-taking for yourself and the parents.

_____Allow enough time for chatty parents.

_____Allow time for answering questions from parents.

_____Toward the end of the conference, review key points and present them to the parents.

_____End the conference with a plan of future actions and ways to help the child.

Letter to Parents

Dear Families,

It is time to schedule our annual conference. I am allotting a time slot for each child. However, it is not a mandatory meeting, and if you prefer not to have a conference, please check the box below.

Available time slots are as follows:

Time	Date

Please return this slip to me by _____ .

Thank you,

_____

- -

❏ Yes, I would like to have a conference.

  • My first choice for a conference time and date is:

  • My second choice for a conference time and date is:

❏ Yes, I would like to have a conference, but I am unable to come at any of the available times. Please call me to arrange another time. My number is _____ .

❏ I do not feel my child needs a conference at this time.

Parent _____

Parent Conference Notes

Date_____

Child_____

Parents _____

Purpose of conference _____

We discussed the following points:

The parents would like

We have planned

Signed _____

Preschool Questionnaire

Child's name _____

Parents' names _____

Address _____

Phone number _____ Birthday _____

My child is special because _____

_____

_____

_____

Foods that I do not want my child to eat are _____

_____

Allergies my child has are _____

_____

A talent/skill that I can share with the class/teacher is _____

_____

❑ I would like to be a room parent/volunteer.

❑ I can drive on field trips. I have_____ seatbelts for passengers.

More Ideas

There are many ideas in this section of the book, and they are sure to inspire ideas of your own. Use this form to jot down your notes and the helpful ideas you hear from your colleagues.

My Ideas for Parent Conferences

We must see that every child has equal opportunity not to become equal, but to become different—to realize the unique potential he or she possesses.

—*John Fischer*

What Is Inclusion?

In 1975, the 94th Congress passed a federal law known as Public Law 94–142 or the Education for All Handicapped Children Law. The basis of the law states, ". . . a free, appropriate, public education . . . to all handicapped children between the ages of three and twenty-one by no later than September of 1980." Thus began the influx of children with handicaps into the public school. The term "inclusion" soon began to become a household name in many school programs. Inclusion is exactly what it sounds like: including children with special needs, side by side, with their non-handicapped peers. The children learn from each other. The research tells us over and over again about the benefits of inclusion. Inclusion in early intervention can, in some cases, prevent developmental problems, result in fewer children being retained in later grades, reduce educational costs to school programs, and improve the quality of family relationships.

The most recent trend has been to remove the child with handicaps from the traditional special school setting and include him or her into a public or private preschool setting. An itinerant special education teacher may assist you and support you with training and intervention techniques, but only on a part-time basis.

A true inclusion program has more than one child with handicaps in a classroom of seven to eight children of normal development. This depends, of course, on the teacher-child ratio and the degree to which the program must be modified around the child's needs.

Modifications

Answer these questions when looking to enroll a child with special needs.
- What kind of modifications are expected of a center when a child with handicaps enrolls?
- Look at the room arrangement. Will it accommodate adaptive equipment?
- What are the ages of the other students in your class?
- What other special needs are in the classroom?
- What is the teacher-child ratio?
- What kinds of support are you able to get from school district teachers and therapists?
- Will this child be able to play on the playground?
- What is the child's developmental delay?
- Do you understand the perimeters of the disability?
- Does your staff need extra training to include this child?
- Do you have any resources for training to include this child?
- Have the parents and child visited the school or center?
- Has the center met in a cooperative meeting with all parties involved with this child (therapists, teachers, special education teachers, parents) so that everyone knows what goals are planned and how they will go about meeting them?

When you answer these questions, it will be obvious if you are ready to include the child into your program. If you are not ready to accept this child, please be honest with the parents. If you accept this child and he/she cannot be included appropriately, then you are wasting the precious developmental learning time of the child. Inclusion done correctly is priceless in its effects on the children it touches.

Terms and Definitions

Here are some terms and definitions that are associated with inclusion. You may encounter one or more of these when a child with developmental delays is included into your program.

Autism: This is a neurological condition in which the child may have severe problems in communication and behavior. These children are usually unable to relate to adults or other children in a normal way. Characteristics of autism include avoiding eye contact, poor social relationships, exhibiting repetitive or non-compliant behavior, having abnormal responses to sensory stimulation, impaired general intellectual functions, and having speech and language difficulties.

Cerebral Palsy: This is an injury to the brain which effects the controls of movement in the body. The severity depends on how much damage occurred and which area of the brain was affected. Some children may feel "floppy" and have low muscle tone, while some may have stiff and tense muscles and/or have involuntary movement.

Communication Disorder: This is an impairment involving problems with speaking or understanding.

Developmentally Appropriate Practice: This is a way of thinking and working with children. It is two-dimensional: It is age appropriate and individually-appropriate at the same time. It is child-initiated, child-directed, and teacher-supported play, providing for all areas of development.

Developmental Disability: Conditions including mental handicap, cerebral palsy, autism, spina bifida, and epilepsy, all of which may affect the development of the child. Such a disability is manifested before the age of twenty-two.

Established Conditions: This is a diagnosis that has a high probability of resulting in a disability or delay such as a genetic disorder or neurological condition.

Inclusion: This means to include all children in normal activities with each another.

Least Restrictive Environment (LRE): This is the part of federal law 94–142 that deals with placing children with disabilities, to the maximum extent appropriate, with children who do not have disabilities.

Mental Handicap: This is an overall slowness in cognitive development and intellectual ability. In a mild state, the child is slower than other children in learning and may need extra assistance in learning tasks. In a moderate state, the child may be clumsy and delayed in speech and motor skills. These children behave like a child half their chronological age. Tasks need to be broken down into small steps.

Severe/Profound: This means that the child will require assistance in all daily care skills. Tasks must be taught in small repetitious steps. The child may have special feeding and movement difficulties.

Terms and Definitions (cont.)

Occupational Therapy: This includes services to improve self-help skills, adaptive behavior, play, and sensory-motor and postural development. The services include identification, assessment, and intervention. Intervention includes the adaptation of the environment and selection, design, and therapeutic devices to facilitate self-help skills.

Physical Therapy: Includes screening of infants and toddlers to identify movement or motor problems (crawling, sitting, walking), obtaining, interpreting, and integrating information appropriate to program planning, and providing therapy to facilitate motor skills to alleviate pain and prevent the onset of a disease or disability.

Psychological Services: These include the administration of psychological and developmental tests and other assessment procedures to interpret, obtain, and integrate information about behavior. These services also can include information pertaining to the child and family conditions related to learning, mental health, and development. Included in this are psychological counseling for children and parents, family counseling, consultation on child development, parent training, and educational programs.

Referral: This is the point at which the family or teacher contacts a public agency requesting early intervention services for a child.

Social Work Services: Such services include making home visits to assess a child's living condition and the patterns of parent-child interaction. Social services provide individual and family group counseling, working with problems in a child's family and living situation.

Speech-Language Services: These include the identification of children with communicative and speech disorders and delays in the development of communication skills. Included in this are the diagnosis, referral, and provision of therapies to enhance communication skills.

Vision Services: These are specialized services for children who are blind or visually impaired.

Working with a Therapist

Here are some things a therapist would work on in a school setting and the educational outcomes that might be expected.

- **Positioning** helps a child to maintain an upright position as needed to participate in activities and daily routines in school.

- **Gross Motor** therapy helps a child move from one location to another within the classroom and or school.

- **Fine Motor** therapy helps a child with the grasping, manipulating, and releasing of objects. This includes using tools and utensils in writing, drawing, cutting, eating, buttoning, and zipping of clothes.

- **Oral Motor** therapy helps a child with eating and drinking, production of sounds for speech, and coordinating breathing with talking and eating.

- **Visual Motor** therapy helps a child visually to guide his or her hand in classroom tasks for producing shapes and letters by size, shape, and color and for coloring and handwriting.

- **Attention** therapy helps a child with attention difficulties to concentrate on classroom tasks. This also helps in transitioning a child from one task to another.

- **Sequencing** therapy helps a child to plan actions and ideas. It helps him or her to know when to ask for help, and it helps him or her to understand learning routines. Beginning problem solving starts here.

- **Spatial/temporal** therapy helps a child to understand the layout of the classroom and school environment. A child can then learn when and where activities take place.

- **Adaptive Behavior** therapy helps with social interaction and establishing relationships.

- **Language** therapy helps a child to understand language by demonstrating thoughts and ideas through speech, signs, drawing, or word processing.

How the Therapist Can Help

The whole basis of inclusion is to work with a child who may have developmental delays or challenges, to get him or her to learn side-by-side with his/her non-handicapped peers. This means that sometimes you are not only including the child into a group, but including a therapist as well. This should always be planned in advance so that the therapist is aware of your goals for the lesson. The therapist can guide you in working on therapy goals with the child when the therapist is not present. This may be something to work on in art, outside play, or circle time. For example, take positioning. If Sarah has a difficult time maintaining her posture in a chair and sits much better on the floor, the therapist can show you ways that she can sit in circle time that will enhance her attention. Once she is sitting without worrying about falling over, she can attend to the lesson at hand much better.

Checklist for Therapist Referral

Each year the makeup of your class is very different. You will have children who are shy, aggressive, quiet, loud, impulsive, reserved, coordinated, awkward, passive, and active. Some will speak in sentences; some children will only use short phrases. There may be some children who will seem to you to be somewhat delayed. When you use the developmental checklist you will find areas that may point to a concern.

Here is a checklist that will help you to decide if there should be some intervention by an occupational or physical therapist. Remember that you are not a diagnostician. Gently bring up your concerns to the parents and have them take the checklist to their pediatrician to make a final referral.

Pre-K Checklist

Please check all that apply.

- ❏ Does not have fun on the playground.
- ❏ Stumbles and falls more frequently than others his age.
- ❏ Has a hard time keeping his/her balance in games.
- ❏ Throwing or catching a ball seem difficult.
- ❏ Large movements are clumsy.
- ❏ Has splints, braces, or other adaptive equipment.
- ❏ Walks on his/her toes.
- ❏ Feels heavy or stiff when I try to help him/her position his/her body.
- ❏ Has extreme tightness at any joint, limiting function.
- ❏ Becomes easily tired.
- ❏ Walks or runs into furniture or walls.
- ❏ Is unable to walk.
- ❏ Sitting posture is poor.
- ❏ Dislikes having others standing or working nearby.
- ❏ Has trouble holding head up when sitting.
- ❏ Appears weak.
- ❏ Has low muscle tone.
- ❏ Becomes anxious when feet leave the ground.

Maximizing Inclusion

Inclusion involves all children working together in normal activities. Inclusion allows the child with speech/language impairments, developmental delays, mental handicaps, emotional handicaps, and/or physical handicaps to interact with developmentally normal children. The non-handicapped child becomes a role model in all areas of development, but especially in developing social and language skills.

Inclusion encourages children to play together, to problem solve together, to develop respect for the differences of others, and to develop compassion toward others. Inclusion provides children opportunities to use and expand "normal" aspects of their development as they work to remediate the areas of their deficiencies. Inclusion has the potential to create a more demanding environment and to set more realistic expectations for the child with handicaps. Imitation is how children learn, and beginning with non-handicapped peers allows a child to model behavior they see and hear in daily activities.

Education is a way in which we transfer social values from one generation to another generation. We can alter social attitudes toward handicapped children through inclusion. We can help the child with handicaps to feel included in life. The interactions among children with and without handicaps are essential for growth and development. We can also change the attitudes of parents with normally developing children and parents whose children have handicaps by seeing all children as children first and seeing what a child can do rather than what a child cannot do.

Here are some general guidelines and ideas to include children with disabilities:

- Place a child with disabilities in a group as close to his or her age as possible.

- Do not exclude the child from participating in any activity.

- Welcome special educators and therapists into the classroom. They can offer helpful suggestions for each situation, or they can offer necessary resources and equipment.

- When a child needs to have a diaper change or be toileted, provide him/her with privacy.

- Make provisions outside if the child lacks mobility (such as special swings, a quilt or mat to lie on, toys placed within reach, etc.).

- Sometimes special equipment is not available, but things in the room can be used. Rolled up towels can be used to prop up a child or to give support in a chair. Heavy cardboard boxes can be used to support a child's feet during "chair" activities.

- If a child has trouble eating, he or she still needs to sit and eat with the others. Perhaps an adult can sit beside the child and help the child to eat.

- During times of transition, sometimes extra assistance is needed. Quite often peers or a designated adult can help. The helper could, for example, provide a hearing-impaired child with a visual cue like blinking lights or a visually-impaired child with a bell sound to signal a transition time.

Room Arrangement and Materials

Children with disabilities and non-disabled children will benefit when the room is arranged to encourage independence.

- Equip bathrooms with stepping stools and stabilizing bars so children can participate in toileting and hand-washing activities with minimal assistance.

- Place materials on open shelves so children can select them without help. Place some materials low enough so children who do not stand can have access to them.

- If you have children with severe visual disabilities, keep the room arrangement as consistent as possible. If you change anything, be sure to tell and show the child what changes you have made. You can use tactile markers (e.g., fuzzy or rough materials) to identify different sections in the room (e.g., doors, bathrooms, toy shelves).

- If you have children who use wheelchairs or walkers, arrange the room with enough space between furniture so that the child can have access to all areas of the room. Minimize the use of throw rugs.

- If you have children with behavior difficulties, arrange the room to allow for quiet time and time away from the other children.

- Store special equipment that is not being used out of sight.

- Minimize crowding in different areas of the room. If too many children are in the same area at one time, behavior problems may occur.

- Select materials that encourage children to play together. Dramatic play activities, balls, wagons, blocks, telephones, puppets, doll houses, and more all promote social interactions.

- Provide duplicates of toys so that children with and without disabilities can learn by imitating each other.

- Arrange seating during activities so that children with and without disabilities may sit next to one another. Avoid sitting all children with disabilities next to each other or at the same end of a table.

- Include books featuring children with disabilities in your book corner.

Facilitating Interaction Among Children With and Without Disabilities

The teacher who shows acceptance of children, praises each child's strengths, and recognizes each child's uniqueness sets an example to be followed by all children. In order to encourage children with and without disabilities to accept and befriend one another, do the following.

- Praise the children when they play together, but try not to interfere with the ongoing play. Wait until the children are finished before praising them for playing together.

- You may want to pair children who have different skills and abilities. For example, put a talkative child with a child who is weak in language skills, and place a walking child with a child who uses a wheelchair.

- Allow the children with disabilities to be leaders when it is their turn to do so. Allow them to hold the door open, to pass out napkins, and to be the line leader.

- Respect children by not talking about them in their presence or in the presence of other children. Never introduce a child by his or her disability.

- Respect the right of the child without disabilities to choose not to be good friends with the child with disabilities, but do not tolerate cruelty or teasing.

- Capitalize on the interest of non-disabled children to be friends with children with disabilities. Allow them to help during transition times, have them take toys to the children with disabilities, teach them simple sign language, and allow them to explore adaptive equipment.

- Focus on the child's abilities rather than disabilities. Provide opportunities to showcase each child's strengths.

- Answer children's questions about disabilities honestly. Relate the message that children with disabilities do, indeed, have differences, but they also have much in common with other children. Be sure the answer satisfies the child who is asking the question, help the child to accept differences, emphasize strengths, and show support and respect.

Inclusion Checklist

Use this checklist to evaluate your classroom and the methods you use to integrate or include children with disabilities in the day-to-day activities.

❏ Are children with disabilities attending class with other children of a similar age?

❏ Do children with disabilities engage in activities at the same time as do other children?

❏ Do children with disabilities use the same or similar materials as do other children?

❏ Do children with disabilities make changes/transitions between activities at the same time as do other children?

❏ Do children with disabilities have the same opportunity to make choices as do other children?

❏ Do children with disabilities come to and leave the class at times similar to other children?

❏ Are children with disabilities encouraged to follow the same rules as other children?

❏ Are children with disabilities given assistance by peers and adults only when necessary?

❏ Are peers encouraged to provide assistance to children with disabilities?

❏ Do children with disabilities have a way to communicate with other children and adults in the classroom?

❏ Are children positioned so that they can see and participate in what is happening?

❏ Do children with disabilities have ongoing opportunities to have social interactions with other children?

❏ Do children with disabilities dress in ways that are similar to other children?

❏ Is the appearance of children with disabilities appropriate (hair and clothes similar to other children)?

❏ Are families of children with disabilities included in all family activities?

❏ Are interactions among parents of children with and without disabilities encouraged?

❏ Are special education and therapeutic activities conducted within the ongoing classroom activities?

❏ Have adaptations necessary to ensure the health and safety of all children been made?

❏ Have children with disabilities been given the chance to be the leaders of activities and teacher's helper?

❏ Are all areas of the classroom setting accessible and accommodating to the needs of children and adults with disabilities?

❏ Has the entire staff received training about mainstreaming children with disabilities?

❏ Does the language of all staff respect the humanity and strengths of children with disabilities?

❏ Do adult-child interactions reflect appreciation for the uniqueness of all children?

❏ Do the children's books in the room include books about people with disabilities?

❏ Does information available to parents and staff include information about people with disabilities and mainstreaming?

More Ideas

There are many ideas in this section of the book, and they are sure to inspire ideas of your own. Use this form to jot down your notes and the helpful ideas you hear from your colleagues.

My Ideas for Inclusion

A teacher is one who brings us tools and enables us to use them.

—*Jean Toomer*

All About Technology for Early Childhood

Technology should assist children in learning. It should increase a child's participation, independence, and sense of control. Available to the early childhood teacher is everything from simple, low-tech items to the very complex, high-tech ones. Low-tech items might include adapted scissors and writing aids, eating utensils, and picture boards, while high-tech items might be computers, printers, special keyboards, and touch windows.

Children who have developmental difficulties and physical challenges should still be able to participate in everyday routines, and technology can help them to do so. You need to look at the activity that the child wants to do and then use technology to help the child do it. For example, if a little girl with cerebral palsy wants to play dress-up with high-heeled shoes and the orthodics in her shoes will not allow the heels to remain in place, masking tape can be used to tape the shoes on, and she can play like the other children. Also, if a little boy wants to ride a tricycle but he has trouble keeping his feet on the pedals, you might thread some pipe cleaners through the pedals and around his foot to secure his feet, or you can also use a Velcro wrap. Now the little boy can participate like the other children. Technology can be that simple!

Computers can be a real asset in any classroom, but as in anything else, too much of a good thing is no longer a blessing. First-hand experiences are always best for children, but there are good programs that can enhance a child's learning.

- Infants from birth to 18 months have little reason to use computers. They are too young to make a connection between touching the keyboard or using a mouse and making something happen on the computer screen.

- Children ages 18 months to three years old begin to realize the connection, but a keyboard or mouse is too difficult for them to use effectively, so the software should be responsive to a click of the mouse or a press of any key. Worthwhile software for children this age should have repetitive songs, a large cursor, and a variety of activities from which to choose.

- Children ages three to five years old can take a great deal of pleasure from using a computer. With practice, they can use a mouse effectively. Software should be stimulating, and interactive software is especially good for their ability level.

Use technology when it is developmentally appropriate and to keep a child from experiencing failure or frustration. Use technology to be an equalizer, to develop skills, for safety reasons, and for enjoyment.

Children who are "typical" use technology to make things easier. Children who are "not typical" use technology to make things possible. Technology improves a child's independence, self-esteem, sense of belonging, positive behavior, interactions, literacy, safety, productivity, and environment.

Guidelines for the Computer Area

In setting up a computer area in your classroom, follow these guidelines:

- The monitor should be at eye level.

- Feet should be flat on the floor.

- Use low level light or natural light.

- Make sure the computer is against the wall, but allow for air to circulate around it.

- Tape down exposed cords.

- Keep two chairs at the computer.

- Store the disks away from dust and sources of magnetism.

- Store the disks upright in their jackets.

- Protect the computer with a dust jacket when not in use.

- If possible, have more than one computer available to use.

- Have a printer.

- Use developmentally-appropriate software.

- Have blank disks and labels for saving the children's computer work.

- Place the computer on a sturdy table or cart.

- Keep other technological equipment such as tape recorders, headsets, and songs/stories on tape in the same area.

In determining what computer programs to purchase, here are a few questions to ask:

1. For whom are the programs appropriate?

2. What developmental areas are enhanced?

3. Is the program free of cultural, gender, and/or learning style biases?

4. Can children with special needs use the program?

5. How can the program be integrated during the day?

6. Is it easy for children to use, or does it require adult help?

Basic Terminology

These are helpful terms to know when working with computers.

CD-ROM: compact disc; read-only memory

Compatibility: ability of specific software to work with a specific brand and model of computer

Hard Disk: permanent disk where information is stored inside the computer; space is measured by megabytes (MB)

Modem: device that lets your computer send and receive information over a phone line

Multimedia: ability to combine print, sounds, video, and graphics on a computer

RAM: Random Access Memory; allows computer to store and remember information

Software: computer programs, usually on disk or CDs that tell the computer what to do

On-Line Service: information service utilized via a computer and modem

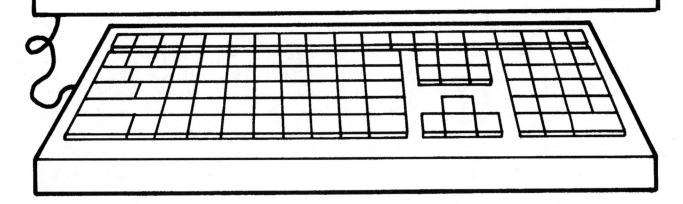

Software and Skills

Listed here are a variety of available software and the skills they can help to develop.

Software and Publisher	Skills
McGee (Lawrence)	sequencing, cause and effect, listening, story creation
Katie's Farm (Lawrence)	sequencing, cause and effect, listening, story creation
Alphabet Blocks (Sierra)	letter recognition, fine motor, directions, cause and effect, listening, keyboard/typing skills, letter sounds, word definitions
Ready, Set, Read (Sierra)	letter recognition, fine motor, directions, cause and effect, listening, keyboard/typing skills, letter sounds, word recognition, word rhyming
Sticky Bear (Optimum)	fine motor, directions, cause and effect, listening, word definition, word recognition
The Playroom (Broderbund)	letter recognition, numbers, fine motor, directions, counting, memory skills, cause and effect, listening, create art/cards, keyboard/typing skills, voice recording, word definitions, story creation
The Backyard (Broderbund)	colors, fine motor, directions, memory skills, cause and effect, listening, create art/cards, word definition
Bailey's Book House (Edmark)	letter recognition, fine motor, directions, memory skills, cause and effect, listening, create art/cards, keyboard/typing skills, storybook, word definition, word recognition, word rhyming, story creation
Millie's Math House (Edmark)	shapes, numbers, fine motor, directions, sequencing, counting, memory skills, cause and effect, listening, create art/cards, voice recording
Thinkin' Things (Edmark)	shapes, colors, numbers, fine motor, directions, sequencing, memory skills, cause and effect, listening, create art/cards, voice recording
Kid Works 2 (Davidson)	colors, letter recognition, fine motor, directions, memory skills, cause and effect, listening, create art/cards, draw/paint, keyboard/typing skills, voice recording, word definition, word recognition, voice/word processing, story creation
Can a Dinosaur (ISM, Inc.)	fine motor, cause and effect, listening, storybook, word definition, word recognition

Software and Skills (cont.)

Software and Publisher	Skills
Grandma and Me (Broderbund)	fine motor, memory skills, cause and effect, listening, storybook, word definitions, word recognition
Sitting on the Farm (Sanctuary)	fine motor, directions, memory skills, cause and effect, listening, keyboard/typing skills, voice recording, storybook, word definitions, word recognition, story creation
Jumpstart Baby (Knowledge Adventure)	reinforces adult-child bond by doing it together, shapes, colors, music, clothing, animals, cause and effect, listening, word rhyme, counting, sorting, vocabulary, memory
Toddler (Davidson)	shapes, colors, numbers, letter recognition, counting, directions, cause and effect, listening, letter sounds, word recognition, word
Ready for School—Toddler (Fisher-Price)	numbers, counting, letter recognition, picture recognition, shapes, colors, directions, listening, memory skills, cause and effect, create art/cards, keyboarding/typing skills, letter sounds, word rhyming, voice/word processing
Jumpstart—Toddler (Knowledge Adventure)	computer mouse skills, letters, numbers, vocabulary, music, listening, cause and effect
Jumpstart—Preschool (Knowledge Adventure)	comprehension, phonics and letter sounds, computer mouse skills, letters, numbers, vocabulary, music, listening, cause and effect
Ready for Preschool (Fisher-Price)	counting, letters/sounds, matching, sequencing, creative, keyboard/mouse skills, following directions, listening, music, sizes, shapes, colors, rhymes
Jumpstart—Pre-K (Knowledge Adventure)	letter order, quantities, problem solving, decision making, social roles, phonics and letter sounds, counting, vocabulary, music
Ready for School—Kindergarten (Fisher-Price)	counting, time concepts, manners, safety, listening, sorting, rhymes, word recognition, music, creative, sentence building, patterning
Jumpstart—Kindergarten (Knowledge Adventure)	letter combinations, reading and sentences, discriminations, sequencing and ordering, counting and quantities, art and creativity, time concepts, comprehension, listening, vocabulary, music
Kindergarten (Davidson)	pre-reading skills, letter combination, counting, quantities, problem solving, time, listening

Resources

Software Resources

Knowledge Adventure, Inc.

1311 Grand Central Ave.
Glendale, CA 91201
(800) 542-4240
http://www.knowledgeadventure.com/home/

They publish *Jumpstart Baby* (9 to 24 months; to be used with parent interaction), *Toddler* (18 months to 3 years old), *Preschool* (2 years to 3 years old), *Pre-K* (3 years to 5 years old), *Kindergarten* (4 years to 5 years old), *Ready for School—Toddler* (ages 1 ¹/₂ to 3 years old), *Ready for School—Preschool*, and *Ready for School—Kindergarten*.

UCLA/LAUSD Microcomputer Project

23-10 Rehabilitation Center
1000 Veteran Ave.
Los Angeles, CA 90024
(213) 825-4821

They have hardware, software, and resources that are effective for children 19 months to five years of age and can be used by children with physical and developmental delays.

Apple Computer, Inc.

P.O. Box 876
Brea, CA 92622-9903
1-800-800-APPL

They have created Early Childhood Connections, putting together hardware, software, teachers' guides, and support materials. They have also created an Apple Computer Disability Solutions Store. The address for the store is below:

Apple Computer, Inc.

Apple Disability Solutions Division
P.O. Box 898
Lakewood, NJ 08701-9930
1-800-600-7808

Resources (cont.)

Technology Resources

International Society for Technology in Education
(nonprofit membership organization; publication: *Learning and Leading with Technology*)
480 Charnelton St.
Eugene, OR 97401-2626
(800) 336-5191
Fax (514) 302-3778
e-mail: cust_svc@ccmail.uoregon.edu
Website: http://www.iste.org

Assistive Technology Educational Network (ATEN)
434 North Tampa Ave.
Orlando, FL 32805-1220
(800) 328-3678
(407) 317-3504
Fax (407) 317-3518
http://www.aten.ocps.k12.fl.us

Children's Software Revue (*magazine*)
Warren Buckleitner
http://www.childrenssoftware.com

Early Learning Software Club (*similar to a book club*)
Scholastic, Grades Pre-K–1
2931 East McCarty Street
P.O. Box 3755
Jefferson City, MO 65102
http://www.scholastic.com

Computer/Technology Vendors and Manufacturers

Broderbund
500 Redwood Blvd.
P.O. Box 1621
Novato, CA 94948-6121
(800) 521-6263

Don Johnson, Inc.
1000 N. Rand Road, Bldg. 115
Wauconda, IL 60084-0635
(800) 999-4660

Dunamis
3423 Flower Blvd.
Lawrenceville, GA 30244
(800) 828-2443

Resources (cont.)

Computer/Technology Vendors and Manufacturers *(cont.)*

Intellitools
55 Leverone Court
Suite 9
Novato, CA 94949
(800) 899-6687

KidBoard, Inc.
7416 Washington Ave. So.
Eden Prairie, MN 55344
(800) 926-3066

Laureate Learning Systems
110 East Spring St.
Winooski, VT 05404-1898
(800) 232-7888

RJ Cooper and Associates
24843 Del Prado #283
Dana Point, CA 92629
(800) RJCOOPER (752-6673)

Soft Touch/KidTech
4182 Pinewood Lake Dr.
Bakersfield, CA 93309
(805) 396-6676

Sunburst Communication
101 Castleton St.
P.O. Box 100
Pleasantville, NY 10570-0100
(800) 321-7511

Public Domain Resources

Center for Adapted Technology
Attn: Kitty Jones
Colorado Easter Seals
5755 W. Almeda
Lakewood, CO 80226
(303) 233-1666

Resources (cont.)

Public Domain Resources *(cont.)*

Creative Learning Choices
1451 Autumn Trail
Addison, IL 60101-5710
(708) 255-9745

EDUCORP
7434 Trade St.
San Diego, CA 92121
(800) 843-9497

Lehigh Valley Easter Seals
Microcomputer Project
2200 Industrial Dr.
Bethlehem, PA 18087
(215) 866-8092

National AppleWork User Group (NAUG)
P.O. Box 87453
Canton, MI 48187

Public Domain Exchange
P.O. Box 70
Alviso, CA 95002
(800) 331-8125 (orders)
(408) 955-0292 (orders for California residents)

Smitech Publications
587 Northfield Rd.
Northfield, CT 06778

Special Education Domain
P.O. Box 327
East Rockaway, NY 11518-0327
(516) 625-4550

Internet Resources

FIRN (Florida Information Resource Network)
http://www.firn.edu

Early Childhood Educator's & Family Web Corner
http://www.nauticom.net/www/cokids/index.html

ERIC Clearinghouse on Teaching and Teacher Education
http://www.ericsp.org/

Yahoo! Early Childhood Resources
http://dir.yahoo.com/Education/Early_Childhood_Education/

Resources (cont.)

Internet Resources *(cont.)*

Cyberbee
http://www.cyberbee.com

Super Kids Surfer for Teachers
http://www.superkids.com/aweb/pages/surfer/techsrfl.html

Uncle Fred
http://www.unclefred.com

Yahooligans!
http://www.yahooligans.com

Cyber-Seuss
http://www.afn.org/~afn15301/drseuss.html

Disney
http://www.disney.com

Magic School Bus
http://www.scholastic.com/magicschoolbus/

Tammy's Technology Tips for Teachers
http://www.essdack.org/tips/index.html

Teachers Helping Teachers
http://www.kinderart.com/littles.htm

Colors and Reading Game
http://www.liveandlearn.com/cgame/colors.html

The Perpetual Preschool
http://www.perpetualpreschool.com/

Nick Jr.: "Blues Clues"
http://www.nickjr.com

The Amazing Picture Machine
http://www.ncrtec.org/picture.htm

TeachNet
http://www.teachnet.com

More Ideas

In your own research and experience, you are sure to come across a variety of technological resources that you will find useful for you and your classroom. Use this page to jot down your notes and the helpful ideas you get from your colleagues.

My Technological Resources

_____

_____

Software

_____

_____

Technological Support

_____

_____

Public Domain Resources

_____

_____

Internet Resources

_____

_____

_____

Good teaching is one-fourth preparation and three-fourths theater.

—*Gail Goodwin*

Getting Ready

A year-end program is a special time for parents, children, and teachers to celebrate the culmination of growth in the children through the year. This is a special time for children to show what they have learned and to receive the kudos for a job well done. Moreover, a successful year-end program is something that everyone will remember fondly for years to come.

The activities presented in this section have all been tested and successfully managed for children ages two to six. All required props and supplies are readily available and inexpensive. The decorations are adaptable to many settings and include art made by the children themselves.

If you have learned and grown with the children, as you most definitely have, these year-end programs make wonderful ways to celebrate the year and the experiences you all have shared. Who could ask for more? Enjoy!

Resources

The following are a variety of resources that will help with any year-end program.

Supplies:

- Polyline Corporation
  (Midwest) 1401 Estes Avenue, Elk Grove Village, Il 60067-5405
  (West coast) 16014 A Adelante Street, Irwindale, CA 91702
  1-800-701-7689; Fax 1-800-816-3330

(This company sells blank cassettes that range from six to 100 minutes per tape. These are perfect for taping songs the children will need to learn or for recording their performances.)

Music:

- London Philharmonic Orchestra. *Elgar: Enigma Variation Pomp and Circumstance Marches, Crown of India Suite.* Sony Music Entertainment, 1992.
- Manilow, Barry. "I Am Your Child" from *Barry Manilow I.* Arista Records, 1973.
- Midler, Bette. "Wind Beneath My Wings" from *Beaches.* Atlantic Recording Corporation, 1988.

Books:

- Branch, Coryne. *Seasonal Punckydoodle Patterns.* Punkydoodles, 1989.
- Warren, Jean. *Celebrating Childhood.* Warren Publishing House, 1991.

Heigh Ho, Heigh Ho, It's Off to Camp We Go!

Suggested Setup

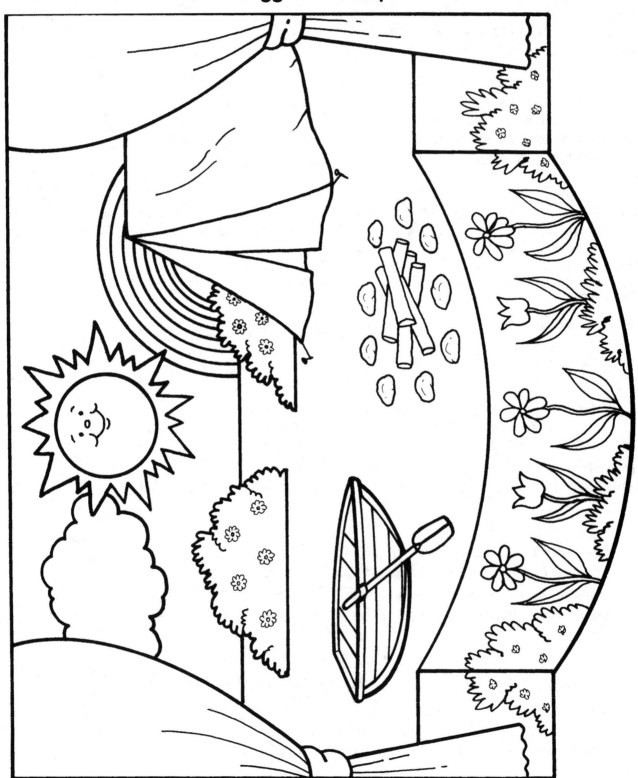

Heigh Ho, Heigh Ho, It's Off to Camp We Go! (cont.)

An exciting way to end the year is to go camping. Turn your stage area into a campsite. (See page 258.) You will need a small pop-up tent, pretend fire, painted paper rocks, bushes, flowers, birds, clouds, a rainbow, and a sun. Directions for making the materials are included on pages 259–263. You will also find an invitation (pages 264–265) and a program (pages 264–266) that you can complete, color, and reproduce for your special event. After your event, send the decorations home with the children. Happy camping!

Rocks

Materials:

- brown paper bags (various sizes)
- paint (gray, white, and brown)
- newspaper
- tape
- paintbrushes

Directions: Wad the newspaper and stuff it into the bags. The bag size will determine the rock size. Tape the bags closed and paint them gray, brown, and white.

Bushes

Materials:

- large cardboard boxes
- sponges
- paint (blue, green, yellow, and white)
- scissors

Directions: Cut bush shapes from large cardboard boxes. Dip the sponges in paint and pat them on the cardboard shapes. Use blue, yellow, and white to alter the green shade. (Test the colors first.) This gives a realistic look to the bushes.

Flowers

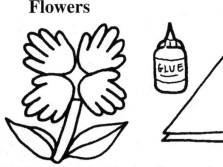

Materials:

- white paper
- green paper
- scissors
- tape or glue
- paint (yellow, red, blue, purple, and orange)

Directions: Paint the children's hands (palms) in different colors and press them onto paper to make handprints. The handprints should look like flower buds with all fingers facing up and close together. Cut out the handprints when dry. Cut stems and leaf shapes from construction paper. Tape or glue together.

Heigh Ho, Heigh Ho, It's Off to Camp We Go! (cont.)

Birds

Materials:

- bird pattern (page 262)
- feathers
- clear string
- hole punch
- paint
- glue
- scissors
- fishing line

Directions: Trace and cut out the bird pattern. Dip feathers in paint and use the feathers as you would a paintbrush to paint the bird pattern in a variety of colors. Take fresh, clean feathers and glue these to the pattern when the paint is dry. Punch a hole at the top of the bird for hanging with fishing line.

Clouds

Materials:

- cloud pattern (page 263)
- glue
- cotton balls
- fishing line
- white poster board
- paintbrushes
- scissors
- hole punch

Directions: Enlarge the cloud pattern onto white poster board. (Do not substitute construction paper for the poster board—it is not heavy enough to maintain its shape once it is hung.) Cut out. Have the children "paint" the glue onto the clouds with a paintbrush. While glue is still wet, put cotton balls on one at a time. Press them to stick. Let dry. Punch holes in the top and hang with fishing line.

Sun

Materials:

- large cardboard box
- yellow finger paint
- pencil
- tape
- fishing line
- craft knife (for adult use only)
- yellow construction paper
- scissors
- hole punch

Directions: Cut a large circle from the cardboard box. Have the children finger-paint the entire circle with yellow finger paint. Trace their hands, fingers open, onto yellow construction paper. Cut out the hands. You will need enough hands to go around the sun. Attach the hands to the back of the circle so that the fingers represent the sun's rays. Punch a hole in the top and hang with fishing line.

Heigh Ho, Heigh Ho, It's Off to Camp We Go! (cont.)

Rainbow

Materials:

- large cardboard box
- pencil
- craft knife (for adult use only)
- hole punch and fishing line or tape
- paint (red, orange, yellow, green, blue, or violet) and paintbrushes
- colored tissue paper
- colored construction paper
- fingerpaint
- sponges and tempera paint

Directions: Cut a rainbow shape from the box. Color rainbow stripes, using your chosen medium. For a three-dimensional effect, use a variety of mediums to create the rainbow. Hang with clear string or tape to the wall.

Tree

Materials:

- large refrigerator box
- craft knife (for adult use only)
- scissors
- green tissue paper
- green and brown paint
- paintbrushes
- glue

Directions: Cut a large tree from the box. Include the top of the tree. Paint the top of the tree green and the trunk part brown. Crumple the tissue paper in your hand and add the paper to the top of the tree by gluing it in the leaf area. This gives the tree a realistic effect.

Fire

Materials:

- 6 paper towel tubes
- brown paint
- paintbrushes
- red, yellow, and orange tissue paper
- tape

Directions: Place tubes in three rows: three on the bottom, then two, then one on top. Tape these tubes together and paint them brown. Cut out slips of tissue paper in layers of red, yellow, and orange to represent the flames. Slip them between the logs and secure with clear tape so the layers stand upright.

Heigh Ho, Heigh Ho,
It's Off to Camp We Go! (cont.)

bird pattern

Heigh Ho, Heigh Ho, It's Off to Camp We Go! (cont.)

cloud pattern

Heigh Ho, Heigh Ho, It's Off to Camp We Go!

Invitation and Program

Directions: Add any desired information, including your school name on what will be the right flap. Then copy pages 264 and 265 (or 264 and 266) back-to-back. Copy on a two-sided copier, or cut and glue the sides together. Color as desired. Cut on solid lines. Fold on dotted lines.

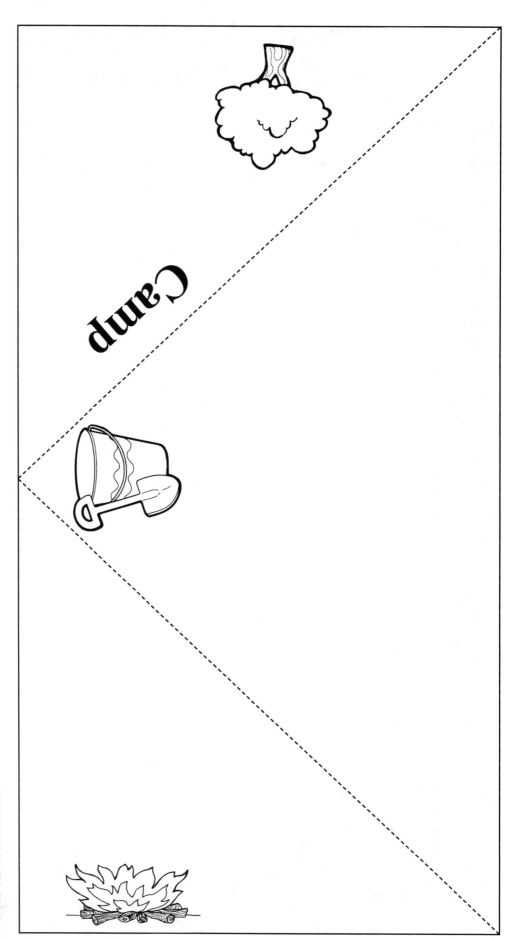

Camp

Heigh Ho, Heigh Ho, It's Off to Camp We Go!

Invitation

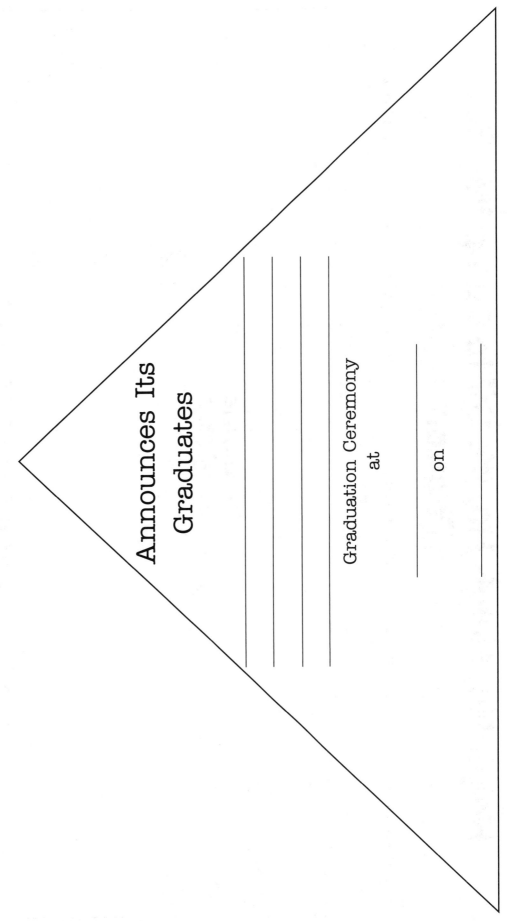

Announces Its

Graduates

Graduation Ceremony

at

on

Heigh Ho, Heigh Ho, It's Off to Camp We Go! Program

Directions: Add your class names on the flaps and fill in your program sequence in the center. Then follow the directions on page 264.

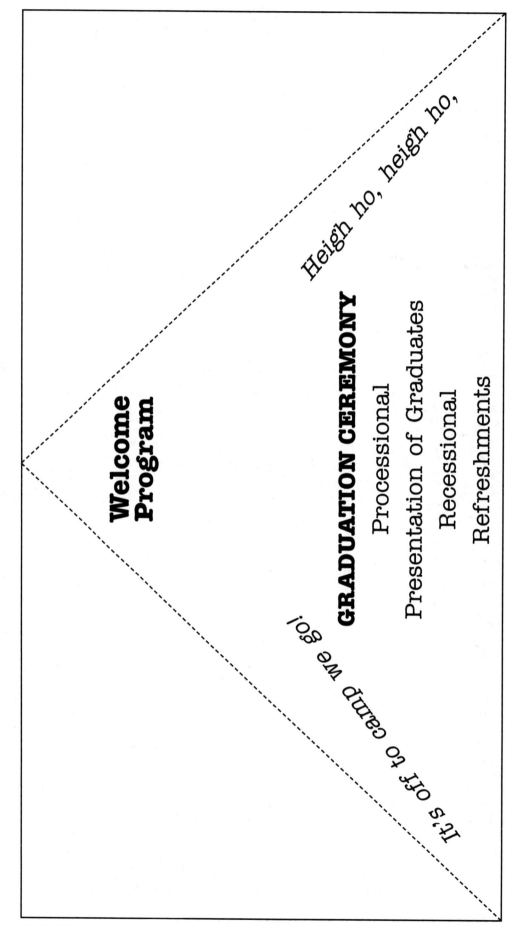

Heigh ho, heigh ho,

It's off to camp we go!

Welcome Program

GRADUATION CEREMONY

Processional

Presentation of Graduates

Recessional

Refreshments

Gift of Wings

Suggested Setup

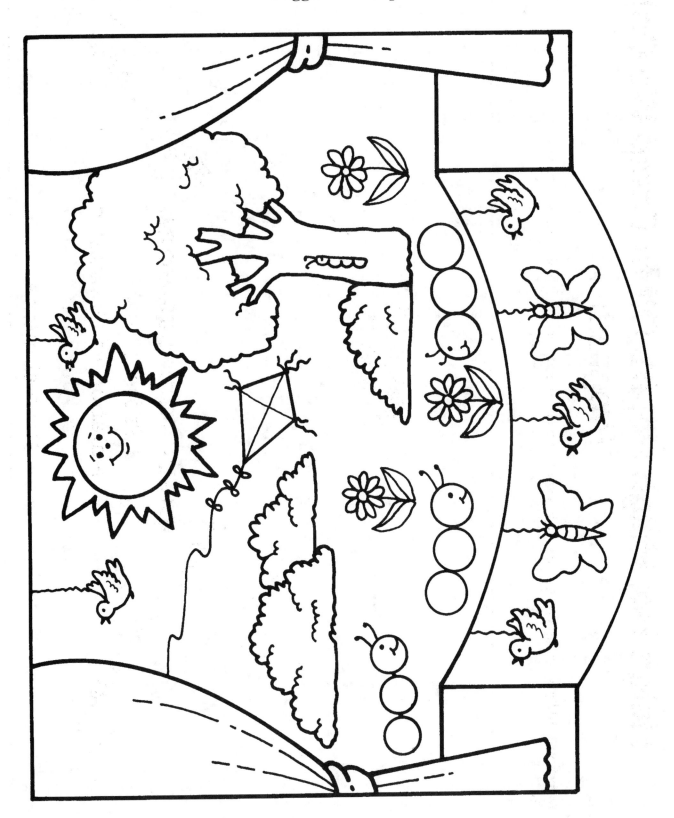

Gift of Wings (cont.)

The Gift of Wings program allows the parents and teachers to "announce" to the world that the children have grown and are ready to spread their wings, moving on to the next stage of development. Here you will find props that symbolize the caterpillar changing into the beautiful butterfly. All the patterns are supplied. A layout of the stage design is included on page 267, and you will find a program and invitation on pages 273–275. Remember to have the children take their projects at the end of the program as they "fly" home.

Zipper-Lock Bag Butterflies

Materials:

- self-sealing plastic bags (sandwich size)
- tissue paper (various colors)
- clothespins (non-spring type)
- black marker
- clear tape

Directions: Wad the tissue paper and fill the plastic bag (one per child). Seal the bag. Use the clothespin to separate what will be the wings by sliding it down the middle of the bag. Place a piece of clear tape to secure the bottom of the butterfly. Use the black marker to add a pair of eyes.

Blotted Butterfly

Materials:

- butterfly pattern (page 271)
- white construction paper
- eye dropper
- various colors of paint

Directions: Duplicate the butterfly pattern shape onto white construction paper and cut it out. Using an eyedropper, drop paint onto one side of the butterfly. Fold the butterfly in half and rub it. Open the wings and you should have a pretty pattern on both sides.

Paper Plate Caterpillar

Materials:

- 3 paper plates per child
- green paint
- paintbrushes
- chenille sticks
- tape or glue
- black marker

Directions: Paint three paper plates green and let dry. When dry, tape them together so that only part of the rims touch. This creates the caterpillar. Attach two chenille sticks with tape or glue to make the antennae, and add eyes with the black marker.

Gift of Wings (cont.)

Egg Carton Caterpillar

Materials:

- cardboard egg carton
- green paint
- paintbrushes
- chenille sticks
- scissors

Directions: Separate the egg carton into the size caterpillar you want. Paint the sections green. Cut small pieces of chenille sticks for the antennae. Use the end of your scissors to poke a hole in the first hump of the caterpillar so that you can insert the chenille stick pieces. Make a small bend in the inserted end of the stick to keep it from pulling out.

Trash Bag Caterpillar

Materials:

- large green trash bags
- green yarn
- scissors
- black marker
- plastic grocery bags

Directions: Stuff a large trash bag with plastic grocery bags. Cut three pieces of the green yarn so that it will tie around the trash bag to separate the bag into three sections. Use the black marker to draw large eyes and a smile.

Paper Plate Birds

Materials:

- large paper plate
- scissors
- paper plate bird pattern (page 272)
- crayons
- fishing line
- hole punch

Directions: Fold the paper plate in the middle. Open the plate. Follow the lines on the bird pattern to create the beak and tail feathers. The children will color the bird, and the teacher will add an eye and draw a wing. Fold in half so that the plain side of the plate is on the inside. Use the hole punch and fishing line to hang.

Bush

Materials:

- large cardboard pieces
- craft knife (for adult use only)
- green yarn pieces
- glue

Directions: Cut a bush shape out of the cardboard. Glue yarn pieces onto the cardboard.

Gift of Wings (cont.)

Tree

Materials:

- large piece of cardboard
- craft knife (for adult use only)
- wood shavings
- glue
- paintbrush
- green tissue paper
- tape

Directions: Make the trunk out of one piece of the cardboard. Take a brush and paint glue onto the trunk. Sprinkle the wood shavings on the trunk. Cut the branches from the cardboard in a roundish shape. Again with the paintbrush, paint the glue onto the branches. Wad the green tissue and place on the branches. Use tape to attach the trunk to the branches.

Sun

Materials:

- large circle box
- craft knife (for adult use only)
- glue
- paintbrush
- gold glitter

Directions: Cut a large circle out of cardboard. With a paintbrush, paint the circle with glue. Sprinkle the glitter on the wet glue. Let dry and then shake off the extra glitter.

Butterfly T-Shirt

Materials:

- white T-shirt
- fabric paint (various colors)
- black marker (permanent)

Directions: Paint both feet (soles) of the child. Press the feet on the center of the T-shirt, next to each other. Add the center body of the butterfly and head with black marker.

Gift of Wings (cont.)

butterfly pattern

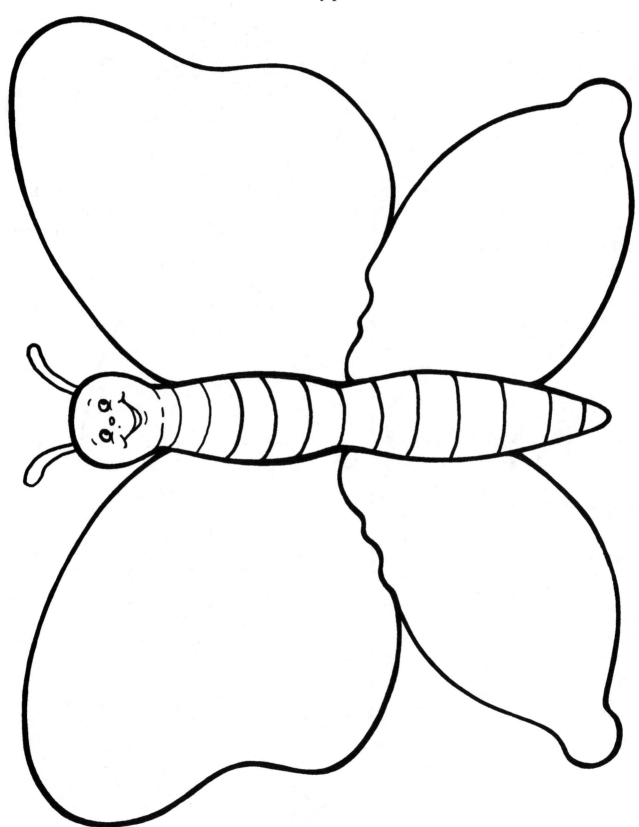

Gift of Wings (cont.)

paper plate bird pattern

1. Put pattern on a folded 8" paper plate.

2. Cut through both sides of the plate.

3. Make a hole near the middle (and near the fold).

4. Hang with yarn.

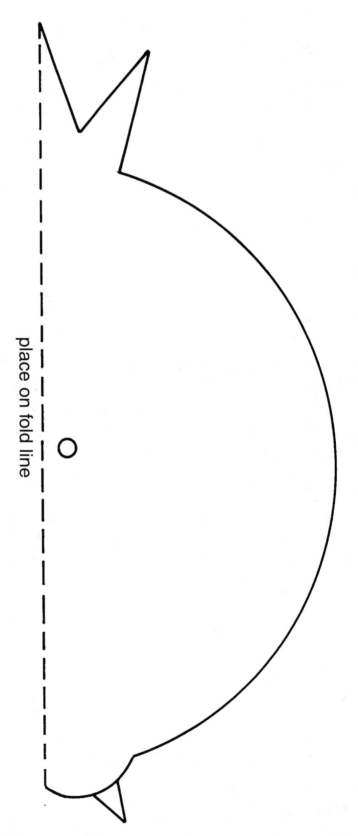

place on fold line

Gift of Wings Invitation

Complete the necessary information, duplicate, color, and cut out the invitations. For a special touch, add chenille stick antennae to the head of the butterfly.

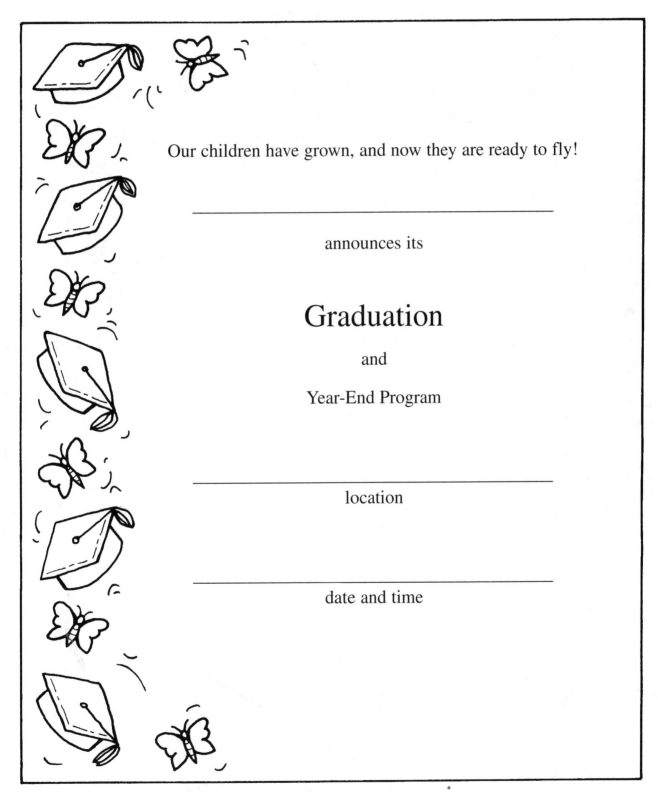

Our children have grown, and now they are ready to fly!

_____

announces its

Graduation

and

Year-End Program

_____

location

_____

date and time

Gift of Wings Program

Copy this page and page 275 back-to-back to create your program. Before duplicating, add all pertinent information including your graduates' names, program order, and any special thanks you would like to make to the parents, staff, children, or other volunteers.

WELCOME
to our

GRADUATION
and
YEAR-END PROGRAM

The
Gift
of
Wings

Special Thanks to:

for making everything possible!

Gift of Wings Program (cont.)

Program: *The Gift Of Wings*

Date _____

Graduation Ceremony

The Graduating Class

Music in Me

Stage Setup

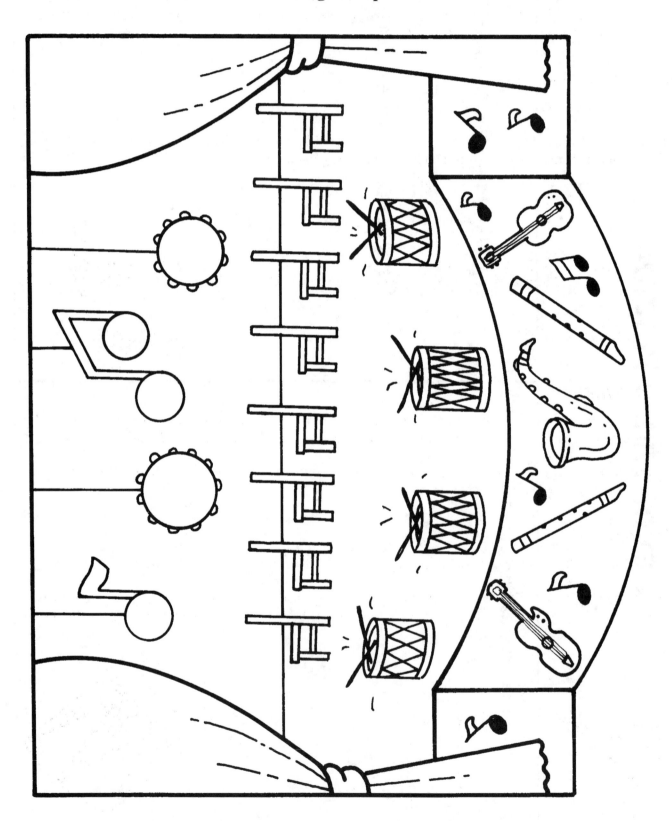

Music in Me (cont.)

This program celebrates children and music. You can turn your stage into a musical haven in no time. The props and instruments that you make for the stage are a wonderful way to send home a souvenir of the night. You will find the patterns for the instruments on the pages that follow as well as an invitation (page 284) and a program (pages 285-286).

Musical Notes

Materials: small paper plates, black paint, glitter, tape, note patterns, scissors

Directions: Paint small paper plates with black paint. While paint is damp, sprinkle glitter on the note. Cut two-inch (5 cm) wide strips to attach quarter notes, eighth notes, etc.

Instruments

Materials: instrument patterns (pages 279–283), paint (yellow, blue, black, orange, purple), overhead projector (to enlarge the instrument patterns), white butcher paper or poster board, pencil, scissors

Directions: Enlarge the instrument patterns, using an overhead projected onto large paper and then tracing the patterns. Paint various colors. Cut out.

Drums

Materials: cardboard oatmeal containers (cylinders), tissue paper, rubber bands, paint

Directions: Remove one end of the oatmeal box. Paint the drum in various colors. Cut a piece of tissue to fit over the top of the box. Remember to have the tissue big enough to hang over the edge of the box by two inches (5 cm). Take the rubber band and place it around the tissue to secure it. Bang away!

Music in Me (cont.)

Shaker I

Materials: paper plates, popcorn, staples, stapler, crayons

Directions: Color the paper plates creatively. Each child needs to make two of them. Place a handful of popcorn kernels in the middle of one plate. Place one plate on top of the other, colored side out, and staple around the edges.

Shaker II

Materials: toilet paper tubes, markers, tissue paper, glue, popcorn kernels (unpopped)

Directions: Color the tubes with markers. Cover the bottom of the tube with tissue and glue (or rubber band) in place. When dry, fill with a handful of kernels. Cover the top with tissue and glue in place. Shake, shake, and shake!

Tambourine

Materials: paper plates, small bells, hole puncher, ribbon

Directions: Punch five to eight holes in the paper plate. Cut ribbon long enough to thread through the bell and the paper plate. Tie the ribbon to secure.

Wood Blocks

Materials: wooden play blocks found in the classroom

Directions: Choose square blocks and bang them together.

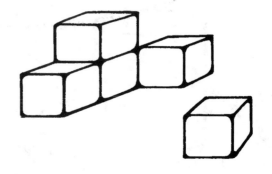

Music in Me (cont.)

Music in Me (cont.)

flute pattern

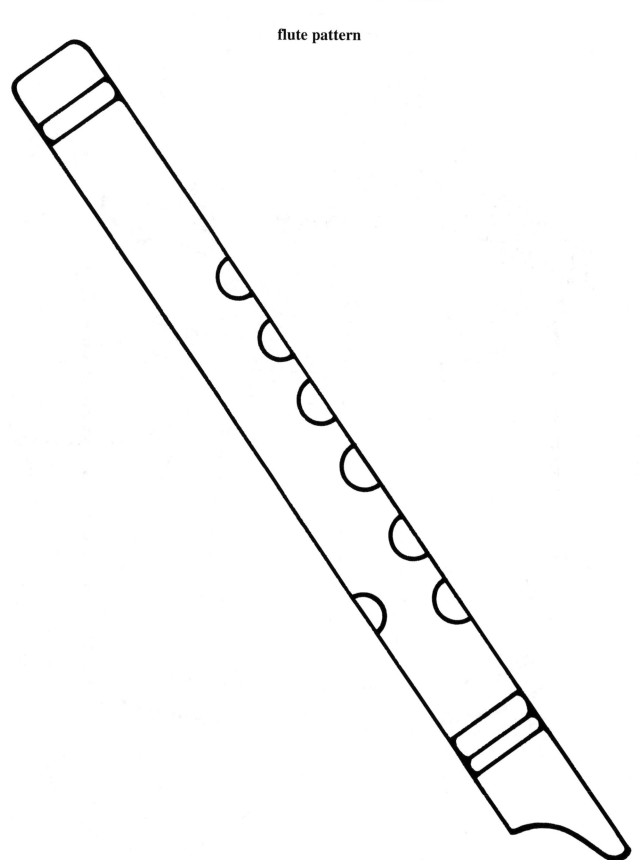

Music in Me (cont.)

saxophone pattern

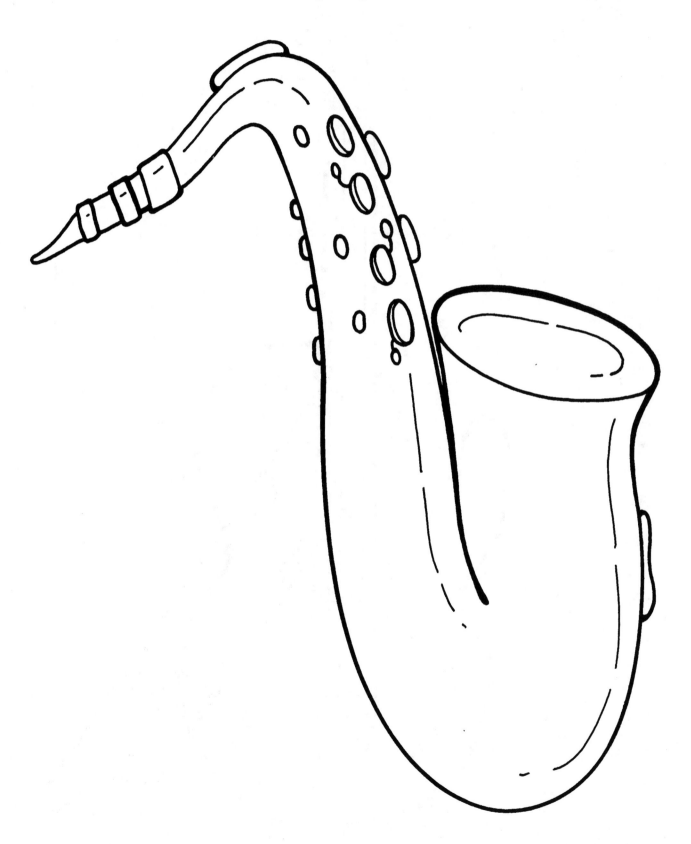

Music in Me (cont.)

guitar pattern

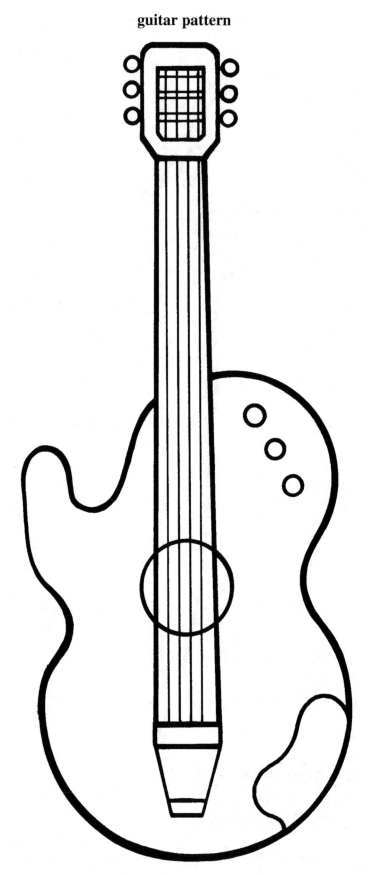

Music in Me (cont.)

keyboards pattern

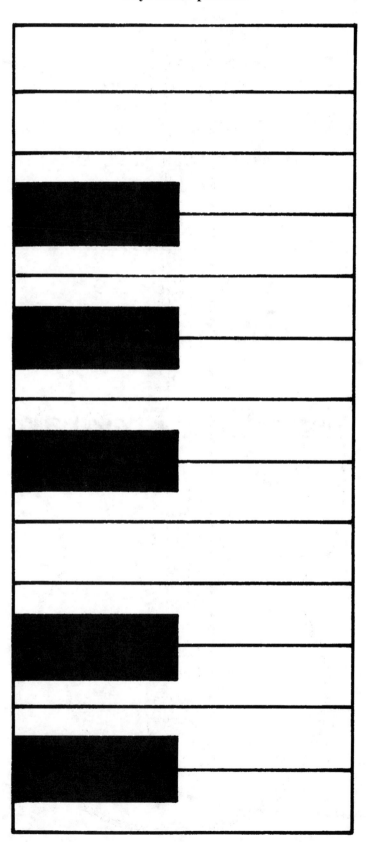

Music in Me Invitation

Complete the necessary information, duplicate, color, and cut out the invitations.

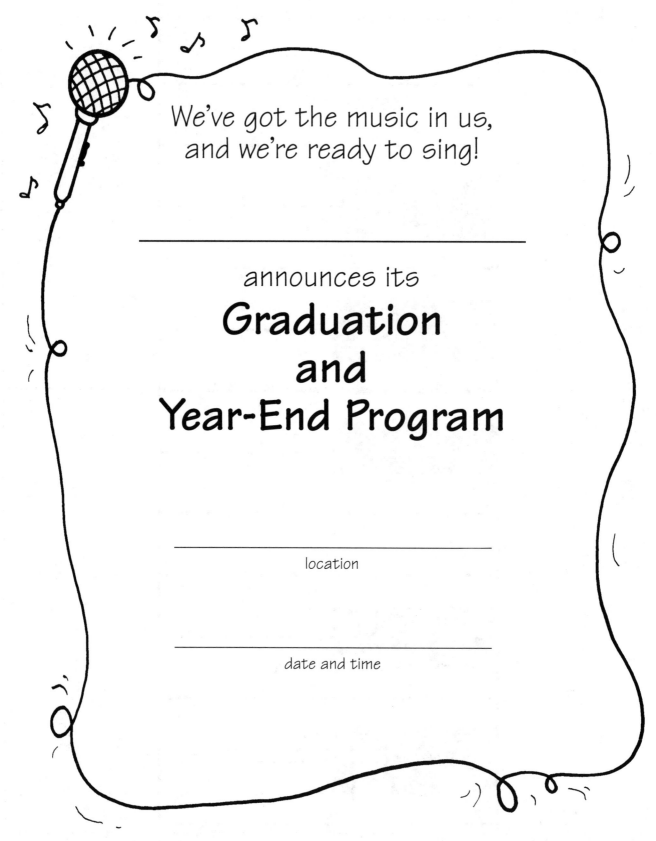

We've got the music in us,
and we're ready to sing!

_____

announces its

Graduation
and
Year-End Program

_____
location

_____
date and time

Music in Me Program

Copy this page and page 286 back-to-back to create your program. Before duplicating, add all pertinent information including your graduates' names, program order, and any special thanks you would like to make to the parents, staff, children, or other volunteers.

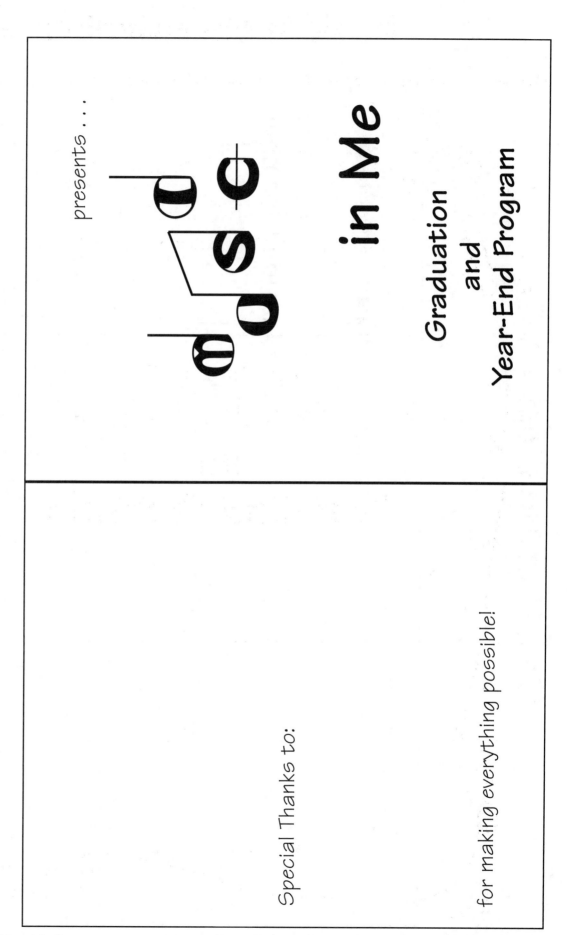

presents . . .

music
in Me

Graduation
and
Year-End Program

Special Thanks to:

for making everything possible!

Music in Me Program (cont.)

Program: *Music in Me*

Date _____

Graduation Ceremony

The Graduating Class

This is to certify that

_____

has successfully completed

the Preschool Program at

_____

on the _____ day of _____ , _____.

Congratulations!

Director_____

Teachers

_____   _____

_____   _____

_____   _____

_____   _____

Volunteer Appreciation Award

Awarded to

_____

on

_____

Presented by

_____

A hundred years from now it will not matter what my bank account was, the sort of house I lived in, or the kind of clothes I wore, but the world may be much different because I was important in the life of a child.

_____

name

You have made a difference.
Thank you!

_____

signed

_____

date

Patterns

Use the patterns on pages 290–301 for student artwork, classroom decorations, awards, stationery, or any other way you can supplement your curriculum and environment.

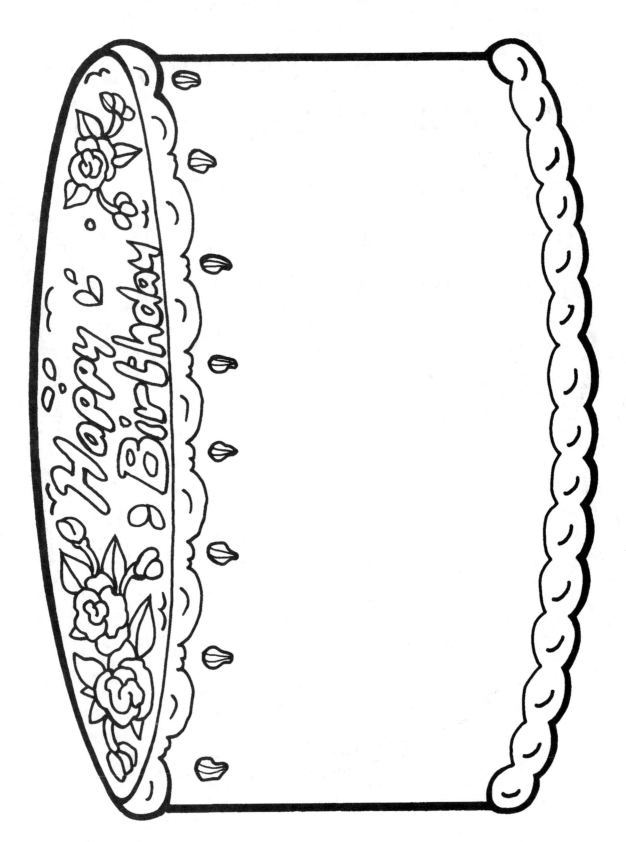

Patterns (cont.)

Patterns (cont.)

Patterns (cont.)

Patterns (cont.)

Patterns (cont.)

Patterns (cont.)

Patterns (cont.)

Patterns (cont.)

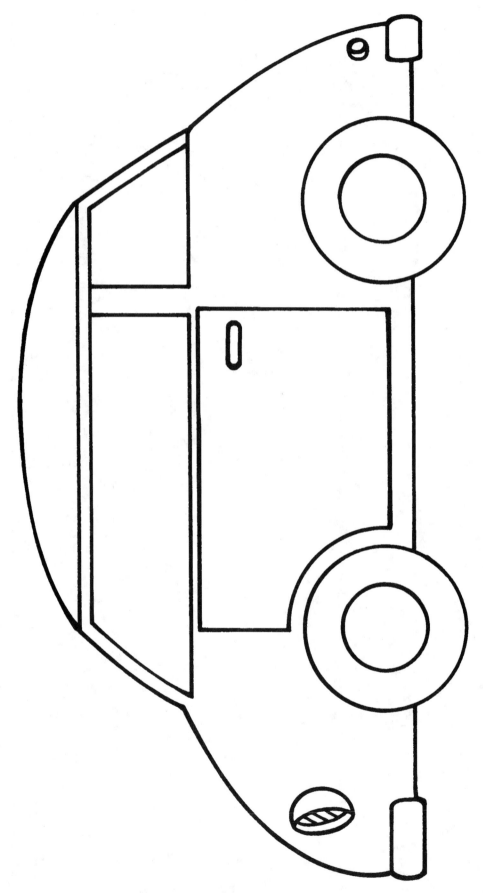

Patterns (cont.)

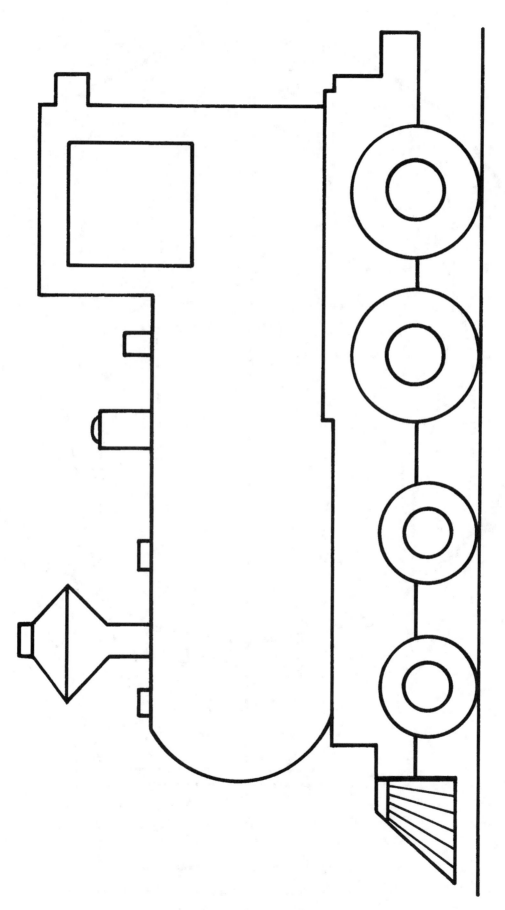

Patterns (cont.)

Patterns (cont.)

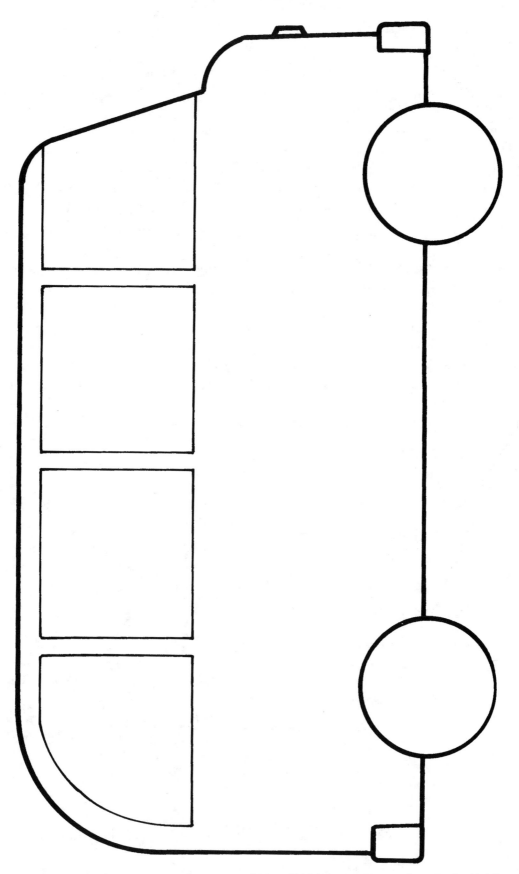

Bibliography of Additional Resources

Ames, Louise Bates, and Frances L. Ilg. *Your Two Year Old.* Delacorte, 1980.

    Your Three Year Old. Delacorte, 1978.

    Your Four Year Old. Delacorte, 1978.

    Your Five Year Old. Delacorte, 1979.

Azrin, N. and R. Foxx. *Toilet Training in Less Than a Day.* Simon and Schuster, 1974.

Bagnato, Stephen J. and John T. Neiworkth. *Linking Developmental Assessment and Curricula: Prescriptions for Early Intervention.* Aspen Publication, 1981.

Brigance, Albert H. *Brigance Inventory of Early Development Birth to Seven Years.* Curriculum Associates, Inc., 1978.

Cole, Joanna. *The Parents Book of Toilet Teaching.* Ballatine Books, 1986.

Donowitz, L.G. *Infection Control in the Child Care Center and Preschool.* Williams and Wilkins, 1993.

Edmark Corporation. *Parent's Guide to Educational Software for Young Children.* Edmark, 1992.

Eisenberg, Arlene, Heidi Murkoff, and Sandee E. Hathaway. *What to Expect: The Toddler Years.* Workman Publishing, 1994.

Furuno, S. *Hawaii Early Learning Profile (HELP) Checklist: Birth to Three Years.* Vort Corporation, 1988.

Johnson, Karin and Barbara Heinze. *Hickory Dickory Talk: A Family Approach to Infant and Toddler Language Development.* LinquiSystems, Inc., 1990.

Johnson-Martin, Nancy M. and Susan Attermeier. *The Carolina Curriculum for Preschoolers with Special Needs.* Paul Brookes Publishing, 1990.

Moll, Patricia Buerke, M.A. *Children and Scissors: A Developmental Approach.* Hampton Mae Institute, 1985.

Uzgiris, Ina C., and J. McVicker Hunt. *Assessment in Infancy: Ordinal Scales of Psychological Development.* University of Illinois Press, 1989.

Wolfgang, Charles H., Bea Mackender, and Mary E. Wolfgang. *Growing and Learning Through Play.* McGraw-Hill, 1981.

Teacher Created Materials

#019—*Early Childhood Units for Holidays*

#020—*Early Childhood Units for Nursery Rhymes*

#201—*Early Childhood Units for Science*

#202—*Early Childhood Units for the Alphabet*

#205—*Early Childhood Units for Music*

#207—*Early Childhood Units for Drama*

#465—*Early Childhood Assessment*

#484—*Everyday Activities for Preschool*

#553—*Quick and Fun Learning Activities for Babies*

#554—*Quick and Fun Learning Activities for One Year Olds*

#555—*Quick and Fun Learning Activities for Two Year Olds*

#556—*Quick and Fun Learning Activities for Three Year Olds*

#557—*Quick and Fun Learning Activities for Four Year Olds*

#558—*Quick and Fun Learning Activities for Five Year Olds*

#860–868—*Early Childhood Monthly Activities (September—May)*

#2008—*Preschool Games: Terrific Transitions and Activities for Your Preschool Classroom*

#2031—*Circle Time Activities*

#2311—*A Year Full of Themes*

Acknowledgement: FSU Center for Prevention and Early Intervention Policy, Tallahassee, Florida, for information on inclusion.

Index

aides 38, 39, 41, 289

art 13, 25–34, 133, 134, 143, 177–181,
259–261, 268–270, 277, 278

anger 214

awards 221–224, 288, 289

balls 132, 134

beads 141

blocks 13, 141, 163

bubbles 31, 133

cars and trucks 141

centers 8, 17, 18, 19

charting behaviors 220

class book 104, 105

cleaning 16, 20, 21, 37

cleaning up *(with children)* 6, 193, 194

climbing structures 135

communicators 55, 103, 106–120, 174, 180, 213, 221–224, 229

community resources 204

computers 245–249

curriculum 93, 94, 96–98, 121, 122, 125–129, 197

diapering 52, 53

diploma 287

disabilities 235, 236, 241

dramatic play 13, 141, 163, 164

eating *(See food.)*

educational quotes 3–5, 24, 45, 66, 92, 131, 140, 145, 157, 168, 176, 183, 196, 202, 210, 226, 233, 244, 256

emergencies 36, 46, 47, 49, 50, 56, 63

environment 8, 57, 211, 212, 239

exclusion from school 60

fine motor 142, 160

first aid 56

floor plans 6, 9, 10, 198, 240

food 169–173

furniture 15

gluing 143

handicaps *(See disabilities.)*

health 48, 55, 56, 58–64

hygiene 52–54, 99

hyperactivity 215

infant development 158–161, 166, 245

instruments 185, 186, 277–283

intelligences 95

internet resources 253, 254

invitations 264, 265, 273, 284

kindergarten readiness 89, 90, 218

language arts 14, 142

manipulative play 14

materials 25–32, 35, 36, 178–180

medication 47

Index (cont.)

modifications for inclusion 234–243

Mozart Effect 184

music 184–194

napping 100, 101

obstacle course 134

oral motor development 170

overcoming challenges 146–155

paint 29–34

parachutes 133

parent forms 43, 49, 61, 206–208, 231

patterns 262, 263, 271, 272, 279–283, 290–301

peg boards 142

play dough 25, 26, 27, 28, 29, 33, 142

playing/talking with children 160, 219

pre-academics 197

preschooler development 67, 79–88, 158–161, 166, 216–218, 245

public domain resources *(technology)* 252, 253

quiet play 124

riding toys 132

rocking toys 137

rules 22

safety 11, 12, 51, 57, 58, 63, 132, 134–138

sample plans 125–129

sand 138, 164, 165

schedules 123, 124

science 14

scissors 143

sensory experiences 25–34, 134, 148–155

slides 135, 136

snacks *(See food.)*

software and resources 248–251

songs 186–194

sorting 141

supplies *(See materials.)*

swings 132, 133, 136, 137

teacher forms 51, 62, 64, 101, 121, 122, 166, 205, 230, 238, 242

technology resources 251

technological terminology 247

technology vendors and manufacturers 251, 252

themes 7, 102, 169, 171, 199, 200

therapists and therapeutic techniques 237, 238

time outs 212

toddler development 67–78, 91, 158–161, 166, 216, 245

toilet training 98, 99

toys 8, 13–15, 31, 132–138, 141, 142, 162, 185, 186

transitions 193, 194, 198

volunteers 40–42, 288, 289

water play 134, 164, 165

your ideas 23, 44, 65, 130, 139, 144, 156, 167, 175, 182, 195, 201, 209, 225, 232, 243, 255